Schwerpunktthema

Abitur Englisch

William Shakespeare
The Merchant of Venice:
Selected Passages

Cornelsen

William Shakespeare
The Merchant of Venice: Selected Passages

Herausgegeben von
Martina und Peter Baasner

Verlagsredaktion
Neil Porter

Layout und technische Umsetzung
Annika Preyhs für Buchgestaltung+, Berlin

Umschlaggestaltung
hawemannundmosch, Konzeption und Gestaltung, Berlin

Photos/illustrations
Cover: Basilica San Marco: © clearlens/Shutterstock images, coins: © Orda Kruglov/Shutterstock images; p. 11: © picture-alliance/Mary Evans Picture Library; p. 13: from Civitas Orbis Terrarum by Franz Hogenberg and Georg Braun, Nuremberg, 1610/© akg-images/historic-maps; p. 19: Ercole de' Roberti: The Return of the Argonauts, ca. 1450–1496, oil on wood, 35 x 26,5 cm, Madrid, Museo Thyssen-Bornemisza/© akg-images; p. 20: The Miracle of the Relic of the True Cross on the Rialto Bridge, 1494 (oil on canvas), Carpaccio, Vittore (ca. 1460/5–1523/6)/Galleria dell'Academia, Venice, Italy/© The Bridgeman Library; p. 23: 'With Bated Breath and Whispering Humbleness', illustration from 'The Merchant of Venice', ca. 1910 (colour litho), Linton, Sir James Dromgole (1840–1916)/Private Collection/© The Bridgeman Art Library; p. 30: © Shakespeare's Globe Picture Library/Andy Bradshaw; p. 38: The Three Caskets (oil on canvas), Robert Alexander Hillingford (1825–1904)/Private Collection/Photo © Christie's Images/The Bridgeman Art Library; p. 45: © picture-alliance/Mary Evans Picture Library; p. 72: The Merchant of Venice, 2004 (Director: Michael Radford, with Al Pacino, Jeremy Irons and Joseph Fiennes) © Sony Pictures/Cinetext; p. 77: Pavel Bunin: Shylock at the Court, 1964/© akg-images/RIA Nowosti; p. 94: John Taylor (attributed to): William Shakespeare, oil on canvas, ca. 1610, 55,2 x 43,8 cm, Given by Francis Egerton, 1st Earl of Ellesmere, 1856/© National Portrait Gallery, London

www.cornelsen.de

1. Auflage, 1. Druck 2012

Alle Drucke dieser Auflage sind inhaltlich unverändert und können im Unterricht nebeneinander verwendet werden.

Druck: H. Heenemann, Berlin

ISBN 978-3-06-033104-8

Inhalt gedruckt auf säurefreiem Papier aus nachhaltiger Forstwirtschaft.

THE MERCHANT OF VENICE

Abbreviations and symbols

AE American English
adj adjective
abbr abbreviation
BE British English
cf. confer, see
derog derogatory
ed. editor
e.g. (Latin) exempli gratia = for example
esp. especially
etc. (Latin) et cetera = and so on
ff. and the following lines/pages
fml formal
i.e. (Latin) id est = that is
infml informal
l., ll. line, lines
n noun
p., pp. page, pages
pl plural
sb. somebody
sl slang
sth. something
usu. usually
v verb
vulg vulgar

INTRODUCTION

William Shakespeare wrote his plays over 400 years ago, yet they still appeal to audiences around the world to this day. *The Merchant of Venice* is one of the best known and controversial. While the play reveals the anti-Semitic notions of Elizabethan England, a country in which Jews were not allowed to reside, nevertheless Shakespeare creates within the character of Shylock a human entity that breaks out free beyond the stereotype to become a full character – part villain, part victim.

It is true that the language of the play is no longer the same as the English which is spoken today, and particularly for students of English as a foreign language there are obstacles to overcome. However, with a bit of help (cf. pp. 6) you will soon find yourself able to understand and even enjoy the sometimes witty, sometimes poetic dialogues and monologues of the play.

Due to its controversial nature, the play is not performed as often as other Shakespeare plays. There is only one modern film of the play, a 2004 version starring Al Pacino and Jeremy Irons, which follows the text very carefully, but includes scenes of open discrimination against Jews in Venice.

The Merchant of Venice is a play made for performance on a stage. This means that the text, while definitely worth studying in its own right, is actually meant as a kind of blueprint for actors. This is why you should try to imagine the scenes on a stage. From time to time you may want to try out some of your ideas for stage directions in the classroom, either as a freeze-frame, or as a more elaborate mini-performance of a short passage.

This book offers a selection of passages from each of the five acts of the original play. This means that your study of the play will focus on the main storylines and characters of *The Merchant of Venice*.

Scene summaries are provided for every single scene in the play to help you find your way in the development of the plot. It is advisable to read and make use of these summaries, because knowing the gist of what happens beforehand will help you understand the way it is told through Shakespeare's dialogues.

There is a list of characters at the beginning; you might find it helpful to copy the character names onto a small sheet of paper you can use as a bookmark while reading, in such a way that you can determine at a glance who each character is.

Enjoy your time with Shakespeare's *The Merchant of Venice!*

THE LANGUAGE OF SHAKESPEARE

Shakespeare's language is not easy to understand, not even for a modern-day speaker of English. Since his time the English language has changed quite considerably, so that many words are no longer in use or have the same meaning. However, Shakespeare remains a great influence today and his words still echo down the centuries, as generations have read and enjoyed his plays. And with a little bit of effort his language can still be appreciated today. The annotations on the left-hand pages will offer you more than adequate help when reading the play. But it would be useful to be aware of some general points before you start reading; so here are a few tips on how to deal with Shakespeare's language.

Vocabulary

While Shakespeare used many words that are no longer in use in modern English (e.g. 'argosy', I, iii, 14, and 'bethink', I, iii, 22), many of the words he used have changed their meaning:

very (I, ii, 17; IV, i, 180)

'Very' meant 'genuine, real, true' besides the meaning it has today.

naughty (III, ii, 18; III, iii, 9)

'Naughty' meant 'terrible, evil, worthless'. Today it is used for children when they misbehave.

Sentence structure

Shakespeare's structure differs from modern English syntax. The positioning of parts of the sentence depended on the emphasis they were given and on the rhythm of the line. As Shakespeare wrote mostly in pentambic iambics, he altered his prose – and often the intonation or pronunciation of words (indicated here by an accent, e.g. 'è') – to make it more suitable to verse. It is worth collecting the words of a sentence and rearranging them in a logical way to understand what the sentence means. Always look for the main verb and the subject first. As Shakespeare liked using clauses, his sentences often seem long and complicated. Note that many of Shakespeare's relative clauses would be separate sentences in modern English. 'Which', etc. is often used to link what could be another sentence onto a previous sentence.

Auxiliary 'do'

In Shakespeare's time, the auxiliary 'do' in interrogative, imperative and negative forms was not always used:

Hath not a Jew eyes? (III, i, 25)	*Does a Jew not have eyes?*
What says this leaden casket? (II, i/vii, 39)	*What does this leaden casket say?*
Lend it not (I, iii, 83)	*don't lend it*

On the other hand, the auxiliary 'do' without any special emphasis can be found in positive statements:

Then do but say (I, i, 22)	*then just say*

Auxiliary 'be'

'Be' as an auxiliary was used to form compound tenses of certain intransitive verbs in Elizabethan English, especially 'come' and 'go' (as is the case in German):

suitors that are already come (I, ii, 14) *suitors that have already come*

Second-person pronouns

In 16th-century English there were two forms of 'you':

- 'thou' (object form: 'thee'; possessive determiner: 'thy', 'thine'). In Shakespeare's time subordinates and children were addressed as 'thou' (in the singular). Moreover the common people (and intimate friends) used this form of address amongst themselves.

  Thou know'st that all my fortunes are at sea? (I, i, 37)
  To spit on thee again, to spurn thee too (I, iii, 82)

- 'ye/you' (object form: 'you'; possessive determiner: 'your'). In Shakespeare's time 'ye/you' was used as a term of respect for individuals ('Sie'), or as the second-person plural form ('ihr').

  How much ye would (I, iii, 52)

However, note that Shakespeare is not consistent in how he uses 'you/ye' and 'thou/thee'. It seems that these pronouns were in flux at the time.

Possessive determiners

In Elizabethan English, 'mine' and 'thine' as possessive determiners were sometimes used instead of 'my' and 'thy' before vowels and 'h'. 'Thine' and 'mine' were also used in much the same way as 'mine' is today (as possessive determiners):

thine enemy (I, iii, 86)

Verb endings

- The third-person singular verb endings: In Shakespeare's time, the third-person singular verb often ended in '-th', e.g. 'doth' (does), 'hath' (has).
- The second-person singular verb endings: In Shakespeare's time, the second-person verb after 'thou' ended in '-st', e.g. 'canst', 'didst', 'camest', 'hast', 'art' (verb: be); or in the case of 'will' and 'shall': 'wilt' and 'shalt'.

Would/will

'Would' often means 'want' or 'wish'.

choose who I would (I, ii, 6) *choose who I want*
I would my daughter were dead (III, i, 48) *I wish my daughter was dead*

Subjunctive

In Elizabethan English the subjunctive was still used.

I were best to cut my left hand off (V, i, 54)	*It would be best if I cut my left hand off*
I would my daughter were dead (III, i, 48)	*I wish my daughter was dead*

But

'But' has a variety of meanings, e.g. 'only', 'just', 'without it being the case that ...', 'except'.

Had I but the means (I, i, 33)	*if I just had the money*
there is not one among them but I dote on his very absence (I, ii, 17–18)	*there is not one who I want to stay*

Adverbs

For a German some Elizabethan adverbs of place and relative adverbs are easier to understand than for a modern English person.

thence [dahin]	*wherein* [worin]
whence [woher]	*wherewith* [womit]
hence [hierher]	*wherefore* [wofür; weshalb]
whereof [worauf]	*whereby* [wobei]

Omission of consonant

In order to reflect everyday speech, Shakespeare would leave out consonants (especially the 'v') in particular words.

e'er	*ever*	*an'*	*and*
ne'er	*never*	*o'*	*on/of*
o'er	*over*	*ta'en*	*taken*

THE CHARACTERS

THE DUKE OF VENICE

THE PRINCE OF MOROCCO **THE PRINCE OF ARAGON**	suitors to Portia
BASSANIO	an Italian lord, suitor to Portia
ANTONIO	a merchant of Venice, friend of Bassanio
SOLANIO **SALERIO** **GRATIANO** **LORENZO**	gentlemen of Venice, friends of Bassanio
SHYLOCK	the rich Jew, a moneylender
JESSICA	his daughter
TUBAL	another Jew, Shylock's friend
LAUNCELOT	servant to Shylock
PORTIA	a rich Italian lady
NERISSA	her lady-in-waiting

SERVANTS, MESSENGERS, COURT OFFICIALS, JAILER

Summary

Bassanio has fallen in love with the rich lady Portia but he has no money. He asks his close friend Antonio for a loan. Although Antonio has no cash available for the moment, as it is all tied up in ventures, he tells Bassanio that he may borrow money in his name.

Notes and annotations

2 *swore a secret pilgrimage:* promised to visit secretly
5 *disabled mine estate:* wasted my money
6 *something:* slightly, somewhat
swelling port: inflated lifestyle
7 *faint:* not very large
grant continuance: allow to continue
8 *make moan:* complain
be abridged: be cut off
9 *noble rate:* wealthy lifestyle
chief care: main concern
10 *come fairly off from:* get honourably out of
11 *wherein my time:* which my behaviour in the past
too prodigal: too extravagant or wasteful
12 *hath:* has
gaged: owing (money)
14 *warranty:* permission
15 *unburden:* explain, reveal
plots and purposes: schemes and plans
17 *I pray you:* I ask you earnestly
18 *stand:* is
19 *within the eye of honour:* honourable
20 *extremest means:* everything I have
21 *occasions:* needs
24 *pressed unto:* ready for, prepared for
Note, l. 25: Belmont is a fictional place.
25 *richly left:* who has inherited a lot of money
26 *fair:* beautiful
fairer than that word: even better than that
27 *wondrous:* excellent
virtue: Tugend
30 *ignorant of her worth:* uninformed about her beauty and wealth
32 *renowned:* with a good reputation and from a noble background
suitor: man who is searching for a wife
33 *had I but the means:* if only I had the wealth
34 to compete with them
35 *presages:* that prophesies/foresees for me
thrift: profitable success
36 *questionless:* without doubt
be fortunate: have good luck
37 *all my fortunes are at sea:* all the capital I have is invested in ships

Act I, Scene 1 (excerpts)

Venice: a street

As the play opens, we discover that the merchant Antonio is very sad for reasons unknown to him. His friends and fellow merchants try to cheer him up. Once alone with his friend Bassanio, Antonio asks him about a lady he had mentioned to him.

ANTONIO *and* BASSANIO.

ANTONIO: Well, tell me now what lady is the same
To whom you swore a secret pilgrimage,
That you today promised to tell me of.
BASSANIO: 'Tis not unknown to you, Antonio,
How much I have disabled mine estate
By something showing a more swelling port
Than my faint means would grant continuance.
Nor do I now make moan to be abridged
From such a noble rate; but my chief care
Is to come fairly off from the great debts
Wherein my time, something too prodigal,
Hath left me gaged. To you, Antonio,
I owe the most, in money and in love,
And from your love I have a warranty
To unburden all my plots and purposes
How to get clear of all the debts I owe.
ANTONIO: I pray you, good Bassanio, let me know it,
And if it stand, as you yourself still do,
Within the eye of honour, be assured,
My purse, my person, my extremest means,
Lie all unlocked to your occasions. [...]
Then do but say to me what I should do
That in your knowledge may by me be done,
And I am pressed unto it: therefore, speak.
BASSANIO: In Belmont is a lady richly left,
And she is fair, and, fairer than that word,
Of wondrous virtues. Sometimes from her eyes
I did receive fair speechless messages.
Her name is Portia. [...]
Nor is the wide world ignorant of her worth,
For the four winds blow in from every coast
Renownèd suitors. [...]
O my Antonio, had I but the means
To hold a rival place with one of them,
I have a mind presages me such thrift,
That I should questionless be fortunate!
ANTONIO: Thou know'st that all my fortunes are at sea;

38 *commodity:* goods on which money could be borrowed
39 *present sum:* ready cash
go forth: go and see
41 *racked:* stretched
to the uttermost: to the highest possible sum
42 *furnish thee to Belmont:* provide you with enough so you can go to Belmont
43 *presently:* immediately
inquire: ask around
44 *I no question make:* I have no doubt
45 *to have it:* that I will get it
of my trust: due to my credit
sake: friendship

INFOBOX Blank verse

Blank verse is poetry written in unrhymed **iambic pentameter**. Iambic pentameter is a line of five **feet** (a foot being a unit consisting of a group of stressed and unstressed syllables that are repeated in a line) in which an unstressed syllable is followed by a stressed syllable (di dum), a pattern known as an **iamb**. Blank verse was first used in the middle of the 16th century and became very popular. Shakespeare varies the iambic pentameter a great deal, while maintaining the iamb as the most common foot. Here are the first two lines divided into iambic feet (if you say 'di dum, di dum, di dum, di dum, di dum' first, it may help you feel the rhythm):
Well, téll / me nów / what lá/dy ís / the sáme
To whóm / you swóre / a sé/cret píl/grimáge.

Neither have I money nor commodity
To raise a present sum; therefore go forth,
Try what my credit can in Venice do,
That shall be racked even to the uttermost
To furnish thee to Belmont, to fair Portia.
Go presently inquire, and so will I,
Where money is, and I no question make
To have it of my trust or for my sake.

Exeunt.

1 **True or false?**

Decide whether the following statements are true (T) or false (F) and support your answer by referring to the text.

T F

☐ ☐ Bassanio has lost a lot of money in a business deal.

☐ ☐ Antonio doesn't hesitate to help his friend with money.

☐ ☐ Bassanio thinks Portia is interested in him.

☐ ☐ Antonio has invested his capital in the Venetian money market.

☐ ☐ Portia attracts so many suitors because she is such a striking beauty.

2 Bassanio is often seen as a treasure hunter. Read what he says about Portia and discuss whether this might be true.

Venice, 17th century

Summary

In Belmont, Portia is not happy with her father's will, which forbids her to choose a husband for herself. She respects his wish, because, as her maid Nerissa says, her father was the sort of man who would be able to set up a suitable test for her to find the best husband. The women mock the suitors who have come until now.

Notes and annotations

1 *by my troth:* honestly, frankly
aweary: tired

3–4 *devise laws for the blood:* invent laws for feelings

4 *temper:* temperament, character
leaps: jumps
decree: law made by someone in authority

4–5 *but this reasoning is not in the fashion to choose me a husband:* but this way of talking is not the proper way to find a husband for me

6 *will:* wish; testament

7 *curbed:* controlled, restrained

9 *virtuous:* morally good

10 *inspirations:* ideas

11 *chest:* a wooden box with a lid to keep the contents safe
lead [led]: Blei
whereof who: whichever one of the suitors
his meaning: the one he (her father) intended

12–13 *will no doubt never be chosen … rightly love:* only the one who really loves you will choose the right chest

13 *what warmth is there in your affection:* how strong are your feelings

15 *Sibylla:* (in ancient Greece) a very old woman with prophetic qualities
chaste: keusch
Diana: goddess of chastity

15–16 *be obtained:* will be won

16 *parcel:* bunch, number
wooers: men trying to marry a particular woman

17–18 *there is not one but I dote on his very absence:* there isn't one whose leaving I don't look forward to

18 *fair:* good and easy

20 *hither:* hierher

23 *foolish:* without experience

24 *deserving:* be worthy of

26 *how now:* form of greeting

27 *seek for:* look for
take their leave: say goodbye to you

28 *forerunner:* a messenger who arrives before his master

Act I, Scene 2 (excerpts)

Belmont: a room in PORTIA'S *house.*

Enter PORTIA *with her waiting-woman* NERISSA.

PORTIA: By my troth, Nerissa, my little body is aweary of this great world. [...] I can easier teach twenty what were good to be done, than be one of the twenty to follow mine own teaching. The brain may devise laws for the blood, but a hot temper leaps o'er a cold decree [...]. But this reasoning is not in the fashion to choose me a husband. O me, the word 'choose'! I may neither choose who I would, nor refuse who I dislike; so is the will of a living daughter curbed by the will of a dead father. Is it not hard, Nerissa, that I cannot choose one, nor refuse none?

NERISSA: Your father was ever virtuous, and holy men at their death have good inspirations. Therefore the lottery that he hath devised in these three chests of gold, silver, and lead, whereof who chooses his meaning chooses you, will no doubt never be chosen by any rightly but one who shall rightly love. But what warmth is there in your affection towards any of these princely suitors that are already come? [...]

Portia and Nerissa make fun of the various suitors from different countries. Portia is determined not to marry any of them.

PORTIA: If I live to be as old as Sibylla, I will die as chaste as Diana, unless I be obtained by the manner of my father's will. I am glad this parcel of wooers are so reasonable, for there is not one among them but I dote on his very absence, and I pray God grant them a fair departure.

NERISSA: Do you not remember, lady, in your father's time, a Venetian, a scholar and a soldier, that came hither in company of the Marquis of Montferrat?

PORTIA: Yes, yes, it was Bassanio, as I think so was he called.

NERISSA: True, madam. He, of all the men that ever my foolish eyes looked upon, was the best deserving a fair lady.

PORTIA: I remember him well, and I remember him worthy of thy praise.

Enter a SERVANT.

How now! What news?

SERVANT: The four strangers seek for you, madam, to take their leave; and there is a forerunner come from a fifth, the Prince of Morocco, who brings word the prince his master will be here tonight.

30 *bid sb. welcome:* greet sb., welcome sb.
30–31 *bid sb. farewell:* say goodbye to sb.
31 *approach:* arrival
32 *condition:* character
complexion: outward appearance
33 *shrive me:* hear my confession (as a priest)
wive me: make me his wife
sirrah: a title used to address a person of low standing
go before: go ahead

INFOBOX | **Marriage**

In Shakespeare's time, women could only marry with the consent of their parents, who tried to match a potential partner to their daughter's own social rank and age. There were love marriages, but usually these would be approved of by both families. Marriage between people of different social rank rarely happened. Of course, the method of finding a husband as described here is purely imaginative.

PORTIA: If I could bid the fifth welcome with so good a heart as I can bid the other four farewell, I should be glad of his approach. If he have the condition of a saint and the complexion of a devil, I had rather he should shrive me than wive me. Come, Nerissa. Sirrah, go before. Whiles we shut the gates upon one wooer, another knocks at the door.

Exeunt.

1. Summarize the information about how Portia is to marry.
2. Evaluate the usefulness of such a test in choosing a potential husband.
3. Explain how this scene is connected to the previous one.
4. Imagine you are Nerissa. Write her diary entry for this day.
   Make sure you mention Portia's feelings about her situation and her suitors as well as your own opinion on this method of choosing a husband and your own views on who she should marry.

Summary

Bassanio wants to borrow 3000 ducats from Shylock in Antonio's name. Shylock is willing to grant this but reveals how much he hates Antonio, who arrives to settle the matter. After arguing and expressing their mutual dislike, Antonio accepts Shylock's bizarre suggestion to pay with a pound of his own flesh if he is not able to repay Shylock in time.

Notes and annotations

1 *ducat:* a Venetian gold coin

2 *ay:* yes

4 *shall be bound:* shall be made responsible by legal contract

6 *may you stead me?:* will you help me?
will you pleasure me?: will you do me the favour?

11 *any imputation to the contrary:* anything negative

13 *sufficient:* having enough money

13–14 *in supposition:* theoretical, only on paper

14 *argosy:* merchant ship
Tripolis: Tripoli, Lebanon

15 *the Rialto:* the financial and commercial centre of Venice

16 *squander:* verschwenden

17 *boards:* Bretter
land rats, water rats: bandits, pirates

18 *peril:* danger

19 *notwithstanding:* in spite of the possible risks

20 *I may take his bond:* I will accept his contract

21 *assured:* reassured; financially secure

22–23 *I will bethink me:* I will think about it

Note, l. 25: Pork is a meat which Jews are not allowed to eat. It would be unusual for a Jew to dine with a Christian, not merely due to prejudice on both sides but also because the Jewish dietary laws would make it impossible to eat the food served by Christians.

29 *fawning:* trying to please

Note, l. 29: The term 'publican' comes from the Bible (Luke 18: 9–14). It means tax-collector. In the parable of the Pharisee and the Publican, a Pharisee and a Publican go to the temple to pray. The Pharisee, obsessed by his own virtue, is contrasted with the Publican, who humbly asks God for mercy.

31 *in low simplicity:* foolish carelessness

33 *usance:* interest taken for borrowed money

34 *upon the hip:* when he is weak and at my mercy

35 *feed fat:* make more intense
grudge: Groll

36 *our sacred nation:* the Jewish people
rails on me: complains bitterly about me

37 *congregate:* come together

38 *bargains:* business deals
thrift: success, profit

39 *interest:* Zinsen
cursed be my tribe: may my Jewish race be damned

INFOBOX | Aside

In an aside, a character reveals his most private thoughts and feelings and shares them with the audience. The words are not spoken quietly though, and it is a theatrical convention that an aside cannot be heard by any other character present on stage.

Act I, Scene 3 (excerpts)

Venice: a public place.

Enter BASSANIO *and* SHYLOCK.

SHYLOCK: Three thousand ducats, well.

BASSANIO: Ay, sir, for three months.

SHYLOCK: For three months, well.

BASSANIO: For the which, as I told you, Antonio shall be bound.

SHYLOCK: Antonio shall become bound, well.

BASSANIO: May you stead me? Will you pleasure me? Shall I know your answer?

SHYLOCK: Three thousand ducats for three months and Antonio bound.

BASSANIO: Your answer to that.

SHYLOCK: Antonio is a good man.

BASSANIO: Have you heard any imputation to the contrary?

SHYLOCK: Ho, no, no, no, no: my meaning in saying he is a good man is to have you understand me that he is sufficient. Yet his means are in supposition: he hath an argosy bound to Tripolis, another to the Indies; I understand moreover, upon the Rialto, he hath a third at Mexico, a fourth for England, and other ventures he hath squandered abroad. But ships are but boards, sailors but men: there be land rats and water rats, water thieves and land thieves, I mean pirates, and then there is the peril of waters, winds and rocks. The man is, notwithstanding, sufficient. Three thousand ducats. I think I may take his bond.

BASSANIO: Be assured you may.

SHYLOCK: I will be assured I may; and, that I may be assured, I will bethink me. May I speak with Antonio?

BASSANIO: If it please you to dine with us.

SHYLOCK: Yes, to smell pork [...]. I will buy with you, sell with you, talk with you, walk with you, and so following, but I will not eat with you, drink with you, nor pray with you. What news on the Rialto? Who is he comes here?

Enter ANTONIO.

BASSANIO: This is Signor Antonio.

SHYLOCK: *[Aside]* How like a fawning publican he looks!
I hate him for he is a Christian,
But more for that in low simplicity
He lends out money gratis and brings down
The rate of usance here with us in Venice.
If I can catch him once upon the hip,
I will feed fat the ancient grudge I bear him.
He hates our sacred nation, and he rails,
Even there where merchants most do congregate,
On me, my bargains and my well-won thrift,
Which he calls interest. Cursèd be my tribe,
If I forgive him!

41 I am thinking of how much money I have available

42 and as I vaguely remember

43 *the gross:* the full sum

44 *What of that?:* So what?

46 *furnish me:* get the money for me

but soft: just wait

48 *albeit* [ɔ:l'bi:ɪt]: although

49 *excess:* with interest

50 *ripe wants:* urgent needs

51 *possessed:* informed

57 *shall we be beholding to you?:* can we count on you?

59 *rated:* criticized harshly

60 *usances:* practice of lending money at interest

61 *still:* always

borne: accepted

shrug: Achselzucken

62 for suffering is the distinguishing mark of our Jewish nation

63 *misbeliever:* person who follows the false religion

64 *gaberdine:* long coat worn by Jews

67 *go to, then:* expression of impatience and anger

69 *void your rheum:* spit

70 *foot, spurn:* kick

a stranger cur: a strange dog

71 *moneys is your suit:* it is money you want

75 *a bondman's key:* the voice of a slave

76 *with bated breath:* with breath held back

whispering: flüsternd

humbleness: Demut

79 *courtesies:* polite behaviour

81 I am just as likely to call you that in the future

The Rialto

BASSANIO: Shylock, do you hear?
SHYLOCK: I am debating of my present store,
And by the near guess of my memory,
I cannot instantly raise up the gross
Of full three thousand ducats. What of that?
Tubal, a wealthy Hebrew of my tribe,
Will furnish me. But soft, how many months
Do you desire? [...].
ANTONIO: Shylock, albeit I neither lend nor borrow
By taking nor by giving of excess,
Yet to supply the ripe wants of my friend,
I'll break a custom. *[To* BASSANIO*]* Is he yet possessed
How much ye would?
SHYLOCK: Ay, ay, three thousand ducats.
ANTONIO: And for three months.
SHYLOCK: I had forgot: three months [...].
Three thousand ducats, 'tis a good round sum.
Three months from twelve; then, let me see; the rate –
ANTONIO: Well, Shylock, shall we be beholding to you?
SHYLOCK: Signor Antonio, many a time and oft
In the Rialto you have rated me
About my moneys and my usances.
Still have I borne it with a patient shrug,
For sufferance is the badge of all our tribe.
You call me misbeliever, cut-throat dog,
And spit upon my Jewish gaberdine,
And all for use of that which is mine own.
Well then, it now appears you need my help:
Go to, then; you come to me, and you say
'Shylock, we would have moneys', you say so.
You that did void your rheum upon my beard
And foot me as you spurn a stranger cur
Over your threshold: moneys is your suit
What should I say to you? Should I not say
'Hath a dog money? Is it possible
A cur can lend three thousand ducats?' Or
Shall I bend low and in a bondman's key,
With bated breath and whispering humbleness,
Say this, 'Fair sir, you spat on me on Wednesday last;
You spurned me such a day; another time
You called me dog; and for these courtesies
I'll lend you thus much moneys'?
ANTONIO: I am as like to call thee so again,
To spit on thee again, to spurn thee too.
If thou wilt lend this money, lend it not
As to thy friends, for when did friendship take

85 interest on sterile money from a friend?

87 *break:* go bankrupt

88 have the punishment carried out according to the terms of the contract

89 *storm:* get angry

92 *supply your present wants:* give you what you need now
doit [dɔɪt]: small coin of little value

94 *kind:* kindness

96 *notary:* a lawyer allowed to certify contracts
seal: sign

97 *single bond:* agreement for a certain sum to be to be returned on a certain day
in a merry sport: just for fun

100 *expressed:* written down
condition: terms of the contract
let the forfeit be nominated for an equal pound: let the penalty be named as being exactly one pound

104 *content i'faith:* yes, I agree

107 *dwell in my necessity:* stay in my miserable circumstances

108 *forfeit:* lose

110 *this bond expires:* this contract runs out
return: profit, gain

111 *thrice three times:* nine times

112 *Abram:* (in the Old Testament) Abraham, seen as father of the Jews

113 *teaches them suspect:* teaches them to be suspicious of

115 *break his day:* fail to pay back the sum on the agreed date

116 by having the penalty carried out

118 *estimable:* of value

119 *muttons:* sheep

120 *favour:* good will
I extend this friendship: I offer this as an act of kindness

124 *forthwith:* without delay

125 *direction:* instructions
merry: cheerful, happy

126 *purse:* collect
straight: at once

122–128 *in the fearful guard of an unthrifty knave:* in the charge of a careless servant who cannot be trusted

129 *hie thee:* hurry up

A breed for barren metal of his friend?
But lend it rather to thine enemy,
Who, if he break, thou mayst with better face
Exact the penalty.

SHYLOCK: Why, look you, how you storm!
I would be friends with you and have your love,
Forget the shames that you have stained me with,
Supply your present wants and take no doit
Of usance for my moneys, and you'll not hear me.
This is kind I offer.

BASSANIO: This were kindness.

SHYLOCK: This kindness will I show.
Go with me to a notary, seal me there
Your single bond, and, in a merry sport,
If you repay me not on such a day,
In such a place, such sum or sums as are
Expressed in the condition, let the forfeit
Be nominated for an equal pound
Of your fair flesh, to be cut off and taken
In what part of your body pleaseth me.

ANTONIO: Content, i' faith! I'll seal to such a bond
And say there is much kindness in the Jew.

BASSANIO: You shall not seal to such a bond for me:
I'll rather dwell in my necessity.

ANTONIO: Why, fear not, man. I will not forfeit it.
Within these two months, that's a month before
This bond expires, I do expect return
Of thrice three times the value of this bond.

SHYLOCK: O father Abram, what these Christians are,
Whose own hard dealings teaches them suspect
The thoughts of others! *[To* BASSANIO*]* Pray you, tell me this:
If he should break his day, what should I gain
By the exaction of the forfeiture?
A pound of man's flesh taken from a man
Is not so estimable, profitable neither,
As flesh of muttons, beefs, or goats. I say
To buy his favour, I extend this friendship.
If he will take it, so; if not, adieu;
And, for my love, I pray you wrong me not.

ANTONIO: Yes Shylock, I will seal unto this bond.

SHYLOCK: Then meet me forthwith at the notary's;
Give him direction for this merry bond,
And I will go and purse the ducats straight,
See to my house, left in the fearful guard
Of an unthrifty knave, and presently
I will be with you.

ANTONIO: Hie thee, gentle Jew.

131 I don't like honest words and a wicked person's thoughts.
133 *there can be no dismay:* there is nothing to be feared

INFOBOX Jews in Renaissance Europe

Jews were settled throughout Europe in the Middle Ages, but suffered from discrimination. Christians believed that Jews were responsible for the death of Jesus and were annoyed that Jews refused to convert freely to Christianity. Many professions were closed to Jews, pushing them into marginal roles considered socially inferior, such as tax collecting and moneylending, occupations which were tolerated as a 'necessary evil' by the Church. Lending money for interest was considered a sin, so Christians were not allowed to become moneylenders. Unfortunately, this led to many negative stereotypes of Jews as greedy usurers and to tensions between creditors (usually Jews) and debtors (usually Christians). Jews were unable to own land and were forced to live in ghettos. In many countries they had to wear distinctive clothing, such as the Jewish hat or a badge.

Even in Venice, which was one of Europe's most tolerant cities in the Renaissance, Jews lived in an enclosed ghetto area (the name 'ghetto' comes from Venice, meaning quarry, which is where the Venetian ghetto was located), which was shut off from the rest of the city at night by huge wooden gates guarded by Christians. The ghetto was small and cramped, and contained the only multi-storey houses in Venice, between which ran very narrow passageways. When leaving the ghetto during the day, the men had to wear a red hat that identified them as Jews.

Shakespeare himself probably never encountered a Jew, as the Jews had been expelled from England in 1290 and were not permitted to return until 1655. Nevertheless, he borrowed for his character of Shylock many of the anti-Semitic prejudices of contemporary Christian Europe.

INFOBOX Dramatic structure

According to classical dramatic theory, a play is divided into five distinctive sections. Modern dramas do not follow this structure any more, but in Shakespeare's plays they are still relevant to understand the pattern of the plot. The action starts with the **exposition** or introduction, which presents the protagonists and the main plot and is then driven forward by the **inciting moment**, i.e. an event which leads to a conflict or problem that needs to be solved during the play. Further conflicts complicate the plot and the characters meet more obstacles in the next phase, the **rising action**. The highest point of tension is reached with the **climax** or turning-point, which marks a complete change for the protagonist for the better (in a comedy) or worse (in a tragedy). The following phase is called the **falling action**, which is usually shorter than the rising action, and contains developments leading to the **resolution** (in a comedy) or the **catastrophe** (in a tragedy) that end the play.

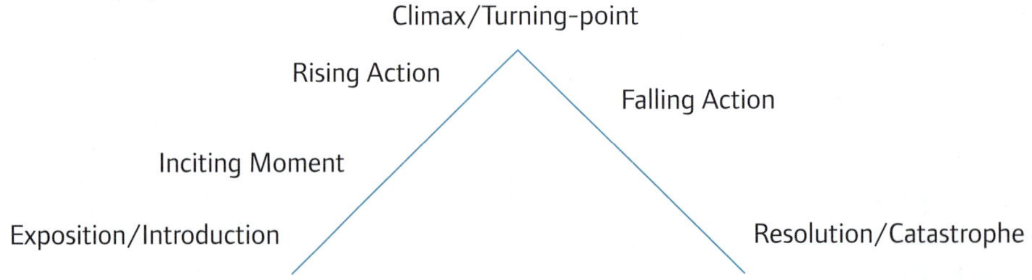

Exit SHYLOCK.

The Hebrew will turn Christian: he grows kind.

BASSANIO: I like not fair terms and a villain's mind.

ANTONIO: Come on: in this there can be no dismay.
My ships come home a month before the day.

Exeunt.

1 The business contract between Antonio and Shylock is the focal point of the play. To analyse their encounters and follow the action and the development of their relationship throughout the play, copy the table below and fill in the information given in this scene, saying what happens, what their feelings are, why they do this, and saying who gets the greater advantage from the bond. This is an assignment which you should continue for later scenes.

Entering into the bond	Shylock	Antonio
Action		
Feelings		
Motivation		
Advantage		

2 Compare what Shylock openly says to his visitors about Antonio's behaviour and money-lending practice with his secret thoughts revealed in his aside (ll. 29–40).

3 Write a short character description of Shylock, examining his method of doing business, his manner of talking (it may help you to say his speeches out aloud) and his dealing with the other characters.

Looking back on Act I

4 Examine the relationships between the characters introduced so far.

5 Explain all the circumstances shown in the play up till now and evaluate the possible obstacles or conflicts that might come up for the characters.

6 Discuss whether your first impressions of Antonio and Bassanio have changed.

7 Look at the 'Infobox: Dramatic structure' (p. 24). Explain which part of the play is the exposition and which event is the inciting moment.

Summary

The Prince of Morocco comes to solve the riddle of the caskets and chooses the golden one because he thinks it reflects Portia's own worth, but he is mistaken.

Notes and annotations

1 *mislike:* dislike
for my complexion: due to the colour of my skin
2 the shaded (= dark) uniform of the shining sun
3 *near bred:* brought up in close proximity to
4 *the fairest creature:* the most beautiful person with the lightest skin colour
northward born: born in the north (i.e. far from the hot sun)
5 *Phoebus:* (in Roman mythology) god of the sun
scarce: hardly
thaws: melts
icicles: Eiszapfen
6 *make incision:* let us make a cut to let out blood
7 *reddest:* most courageous and manly
8 *this aspect of mine:* my outward appearance
9 *hath feared the valiant:* has made brave men afraid
10 *the best regarded virgins:* the most admired young ladies
clime: part of the world
11 *hue:* colour
12 *steal your thoughts:* win your affection
13 *in terms of choice:* when it comes to choosing
solely: only
14 *nice direction:* precise guidance
15 *destiny:* Schicksal
16 *bars me:* forbids me, does not allow me
17 *scant:* beengen
18 *hedge:* einschränken
18–19 *yield myself his wife:* marry the man
19 *means:* method
20 *renowned:* honourable
stood as fair: would have as much chance
21 *comer:* gentleman who has offered marriage
25 *discover:* show, reveal
28 *who this inscription bears:* which has these words written on it
29 *gain:* win
31 *as he deserves:* as he is worthy of
32 *dull:* heavy; uninteresting
with warning all as blunt: with words as graceless as the metal is itself
33 *hazard:* risk
hath: has
36 *withal:* together with it (i.e. the picture)
38 *back again:* in reverse order

Act II, Scenes 1 and 7 (extracts)

Belmont: a room in Portia's house

Enter the PRINCE OF MOROCCO *and his men, with* PORTIA *and* NERISSA.

MOROCCO: Mislike me not for my complexiòn,
The shadowed livery of the burnished sun,
To whom I am a neighbour and near bred.
Bring me the fairest creature northward born,
Where Phoebus' fire scarce thaws the icicles,
And let us make incision for your love,
To prove whose blood is reddest, his or mine.
I tell thee, lady, this aspect of mine
Hath feared the valiant; by my love I swear
The best-regarded virgins of our clime
Have loved it too. I would not change this hue,
Except to steal your thoughts, my gentle queen.
PORTIA: In terms of choice I am not solely led
By nice direction of a maiden's eyes;
Besides, the lott'ry of my destiny
Bars me the right of voluntary choosing.
But if my father had not scanted me
And hedged me by his wit, to yield myself
His wife who wins me by that means I told you,
Yourself, renownèd prince, then stood as fair
As any comer I have looked on yet
For my affection.
MOROCCO: Even for that I thank you.
Therefore, I pray you, lead me to the caskets
To try my fortune. [...]
PORTIA: Go draw aside the curtains and discover
The several caskets to this noble prince.
Now make your choice.
MOROCCO: The first, of gold, who this inscription bears,
'Who chooseth me shall gain what many men desire.'
The second, silver, which this promise carries,
'Who chooseth me shall get as much as he deserves'.
This third, dull lead, with warning all as blunt,
'Who chooseth me must give and hazard all he hath.'
How shall I know if I do choose the right?
PORTIA: The one of them contains my picture, prince:
If you choose that, then I am yours withal.
MOROCCO: Some god direct my judgement! Let me see;
I will survey the inscriptions back again.
What says this leaden casket?
'Who chooseth me must give and hazard all he hath.'

41 *hazard for lead?:* risk everything for lead?

43 *fair advantages:* profit, gain

44 *stoops not:* does not lower itself

shows of dross: things that are of little value

45 *nor … nor:* neither … nor

aught: anything

46 *with her virgin hue:* with her maiden colour, her silvery skin

49 *with an even hand:* objectively

50 if you are judged by how you view yourself

51 *thou dost deserve enough:* you are worthy of very much

51–52 *and yet enough may not extend so far as to the lady:* but 'very much' may not be enough to gain the lady

53 *afeard of my deserving:* uncertain of what I might be worthy of

54 would indicate a lack of confidence in myself

56 *in birth:* due to my background and family

57 *in graces:* due to my manners, my character and accomplishments

in qualities of breeding: due to my good family and education

59 *strayed no further:* did not continue looking any more

60 *graved:* engraved, written

64 *shrine:* holy place connected to a saint

mortal breathing: living

66 *is't like:* is it possible/likely

'twere: it would be

damnation: Verdammung

67 *base:* mean, vile, low

gross [grəʊs]: coarse, of low quality

68 *rib her cerecloth* ['sɪərklɒθ]: cover her shroud (= the cloth in which a person is buried)

69 *immured:* enclosed, contained, covered

72 *thrive:* be successful

73 *form:* picture

75 *a carrion death:* skull

76 *scroll:* a roll of paper with writing on it

77 *all that glisters:* all that glitters/shines brightly

80 just to look at my (golden) outside

81 *gilded timber:* wood covered with gold

enfold: contain

82 *bold:* brave, courageous

83 *limbs:* legs and arms

84 you would not have received the following answer

Must give: for what? For lead? Hazard for lead?
This casket threatens: men that hazard all
Do it in hope of fair advantages.
A golden mind stoops not to shows of dross.
I'll then nor give nor hazard aught for lead.
What says the silver with her virgin hue?
'Who chooseth me shall get as much as he deserves.'
As much as he deserves. Pause there, Morocco,
And weigh thy value with an even hand:
If thou be'st rated by thy estimation,
Thou dost deserve enough; and yet enough
May not extend so far as to the lady;
And yet to be afeard of my deserving
Were but a weak disabling of myself.
As much as I deserve: Why, that's the lady.
I do in birth deserve her, and in fortunes,
In graces and in qualities of breeding.
But more than these, in love I do deserve.
What if I strayed no further, but chose here?
Let's see once more this saying graved in gold:
'Who chooseth me shall gain what many men desire.'
Why, that's the lady: all the world desires her.
From the four corners of the earth they come
To kiss this shrine, this mortal breathing saint.
[...] One of these three contains her heavenly picture.
Is't like that lead contains her? 'Twere damnation
To think so base a thought; it were too gross
To rib her cerecloth in the obscure grave.
Or shall I think in silver she's immured. [...]
But here an angel in a golden bed
Lies all within. Deliver me the key:
Here do I choose, and thrive I as I may!

PORTIA: There, take it, prince; and if my form lie there,
Then I am yours.

MOROCCO *unlocks the golden casket.*

MOROCCO: O hell! What have we here?
A carrion death, within whose empty eye
There is a written scroll. I'll read the writing.
'All that glisters is not gold;
Often have you heard that told.
Many a man his life hath sold
But my outside to behold.
Gilded timber do worms enfold.
Had you been as wise as bold,
Young in limbs, in judgement old,
Your answer had not been inscrolled:

85 *suit:* your desire to marry the lady
86 *labour lost:* wasted work
• *train:* attendants/followers
90 *a gentle riddance:* a pleasant removal

INFOBOX | Theatre in Shakespeare's time

When theatre buildings were erected, they had to be outside the city. They were considered immoral places. The Globe Theatre, which was built for the acting company that Shakespeare belonged to (known as the King's Men), was **a round construction** consisting of **three galleries** around an **open-air space**. It was in this open space that most of the audience stood to watch a play. Wealthier spectators could buy seats in the galleries. Play-going was popular, even among poor people, as it was the only entertainment available, which is why theatres got a reputation for being noisy and rowdy places. The **stage**, which had a roof of its own, extended far into the open space, so that the people actually stood around it on three sides. There was usually an upper gallery like a balcony, from which actors could also speak. There was no lighting, so the plays had to be performed in daylight, and there were very few stage props. This is why characters in Shakespeare's plays often describe the time of day as well as the scenery they are meant to be acting in. Another particularity of the Elizabethan theatre was the fact that women were not allowed to act, i.e. all female parts were played by boys and men.

The rebuilt Globe theatre

Fare you well; your suit is cold.'
Cold, indeed; and labour lost.
Then, farewell, heat, and welcome, frost!
Portia, adieu. I have too grieved a heart
To take a tedious leave: thus losers part.

Exit with his train.

PORTIA: A gentle riddance. Draw the curtains, go.
Let all of his complexion choose me so.

Exeunt.

1 Multiple Choice

Choose one of these three as best summing up the lesson of the golden casket:

- ☐ If you want gold, it means you are looking merely for wealth.
- ☐ If you are not young and wise, you will always choose incorrectly.
- ☐ Most men desire gold, yet it is deceptive as it can cover up unpleasant things.

2 Examine the speech of the Prince of Morocco in ll. 1–12, explaining how it might be seen as relevant in the context of the play.

3 **a)** Describe the Prince of Morocco's character traits.

b) How does this relate to the inscriptions on the caskets?

4 Analyse Portia's reaction to the Prince of Morocco.

Summary

Back in the ghetto, Shylock tells his daughter Jessica to look after the house during his absence, since he has been invited to dinner at Bassanio's place. He is not looking forward to this at all but he leaves in the end while Jessica talks of her plan to run away from home.

Notes and annotations

1 *call you?:* are you calling me?

2 *I am bid forth to supper:* I am invited to supper

3 *wherefore:* why

4 *I am not bid for love:* I am not invited because they like me

flatter: schmeicheln

6 *prodigal:* money-wasting

Christian: (here) Bassanio

7 *look to:* take care of

I am right loath to go: I really don't want to go

8 There is something evil in the making that disturbs my peace of mind

10 *I beseech you go:* I earnestly ask you to go now

Note, ll. 10–11: Launcelot gets his words mixed up. When he says 'reproach' (= Vorwurf), he actually means 'approach' (i.e. arrival). When he says 'conspire', he actually means 'confer'.

14 *masque:* ball at which the guests wore masks

14–15 *fell a-bleeding:* started bleeding

15 *Black Monday:* Easter Monday

15–16 *falling out that year at Ash-Wednesday was four year:* which took place on the afternoon of the same day four years ago, which happened to be Ash Wednesday

Note, ll. 13–16: Having a nose-bleed was considered an omen that something bad was going to happen. Here, Launcelot is making fun of Shylock by implying that a masque was the bad thing that was about to happen.

19 *the vile squealing:* horrible high-pitched noise

wry-necked fife: type of flute which required the player to bend his neck to play it

20 *clamber:* climb

casements: windows

22 *gaze:* look for a long time, stare

varnished faces: with painted faces, wearing masks

23 *stop:* shut

24 *shallow foppery:* superficial nonsense

25 *sober:* moral and well-behaved

Jacob: Jewish prophet who became a rich man after starting with nothing

staff: stick

26 *I have no mind of:* I don't want to

feasting forth: eating away from home

27 *sirrah:* a title used to address a person of low status

29 *for all this:* despite all this

Note, l. 31: There was a saying 'to be worth a Jew's eye', meaning that something was valuable.

Act II, Scene 5

Venice: Shylock's house.

Launcelot, Shylock's servant, decides to leave him to work for Bassanio because he believes the Jew's house is a living hell and Shylock is like the devil himself. Jessica, Shylock's daughter, makes secret arrangements to flee her father's house, too, to become the wife of Lorenzo, a good friend of Antonio and Bassanio.

SHYLOCK *and* LAUNCELOT. *Enter* JESSICA.

JESSICA: Call you? What is your will?
SHYLOCK: I am bid forth to supper, Jessica:
There are my keys. But wherefore should I go?
I am not bid for love; they flatter me.
But yet I'll go in hate, to feed upon
The prodigal Christian. Jessica, my girl,
Look to my house. I am right loath to go.
There is some ill a-brewing towards my rest,
For I did dream of money-bags tonight.

LAUNCELOT: I beseech you, sir, go: my young master doth expect your reproach.

SHYLOCK: So do I his.

LAUNCELOT: And they have conspired together, I will not say you shall see a masque; but if you do, then it was not for nothing that my nose fell a-bleeding on Black Monday last at six o'clock i' the morning, falling out that year on Ash Wednesday was four year, in the afternoon.

SHYLOCK: What, are there masques? Hear you me, Jessica:
Lock up my doors; and when you hear the drum
And the vile squealing of the wry-necked fife,
Clamber not you up to the casements then,
Nor thrust your head into the public street
To gaze on Christian fools with varnished faces,
But stop my house's ears, I mean my casements.
Let not the sound of shallow foppery enter
My sober house. By Jacob's staff, I swear,
I have no mind of feasting forth tonight:
But I will go. Go you before me, sirrah;
Say I will come.
LAUNCELOT: I will go before, sir.
[To JESSICA*]* Mistress, look out at window, for all this.
There will come a Christian by
will be worth a Jewess' eye.

Exit.

32 *Hagar:* a non-Jewish sexual partner of Abraham, who together with their child was exiled for mocking the birth of Abraham's legitimate child

offspring: child

36 *bid:* ask

Note, l. 37: A proverb meaning that what is safely secured will remain safe.

38 *stale:* not fresh

thrifty: sparsam

39 *if my fortune be not crossed:* if nothing gets in the way of my good luck

SHYLOCK: What says that fool of Hagar's offspring, ha?
JESSICA: His words were 'Farewell mistress'; nothing else.
SHYLOCK: [...] Well, Jessica, go in.
Perhaps I will return immediately.
Do as I bid you: shut doors after you.
Fast bind, fast find.
A proverb never stale in thrifty mind.

Exit.

JESSICA: Farewell; and if my fortune be not crossed,
I have a father, you a daughter, lost.

Exit.

Lorenzo and his friends go to Shylock's home, where they help Jessica to escape. She takes with her a large amount of Shylock's jewels and money. When Shylock discovers his losses, he is deeply shaken and almost driven to despair.
In the meantime Bassanio sets sail for Belmont, but there are rumours that one of Antonio's ships has run aground.

1 In this scene we see Jessica prepare to run away from her father's house. In one sentence suggest why she might want to escape from her father.

2 In ll. 11 and 13 Launcelot uses the words 'reproach' and 'conspire' incorrectly (he means 'approach' and 'confer'). Explain why his choice of words might still be fitting.

3 Shakespeare has created two different worlds for his characters: Portia's Belmont (from the French 'bel/beau'= beautiful and 'mont'= mountain) and commercial Venice.
Compare both settings in regard to their inhabitants, their main occupation and the general atmosphere of both places.

Summary

The second important suitor, the Prince of Aragon, hopes to win Portia by choosing the right casket but finds out that the inscription on the silver box does not deliver what he hoped for.

Notes and annotations

1 *straight:* at once
2 *hath ta'en:* has taken
oath: Schwur
3 *election:* (making his) choice
train: attendants/followers
4 *behold:* look
5 *wherein:* in which
6 the wedding ceremony will take place immediately
8 *from hence:* from here
9 *enjoined:* bound/sworn
10 *unfold:* tell, reveal
11 *'twas:* it was
11–12 *fail of:* fail to choose
13 *woo a maid in way of marriage:* try to get a girl to marry me
14 if I am unlucky in my choosing
16 *injunctions:* rules that must be followed
18 *addressed me:* prepared myself
fortune now: good luck
19 *base:* worthless
21 *you shall look fairer:* you will have to look more attractive
ere: before
24–25 *that 'many' may be meant by:* 'many' may be referring to
25 *fool multitude:* the foolish common crowd
27 *jump:* agree, do the same
common spirits: common people
28 *rank me:* place myself on the same level
barbarous multitudes: vulgar masses
30 *title:* inscription, words
32 *go about:* attempt
33 *cozen:* cheat
34 *stamp:* Stempel
let none presume: no one should think of himself so highly
37 *I will assume desert:* I will claim what rightfully belongs to me

Act II, Scene 9

Belmont: a room in PORTIA*'s house.*

Enter NERISSA *and a* SERVANT.

NERISSA: Quick, quick, I pray thee; draw the curtain straight.
The Prince of Aragon hath ta'en his oath,
And comes to his election presently.

Enter the PRINCE OF ARAGON, PORTIA, *and their trains.*

PORTIA: Behold, there stand the caskets, noble prince.
If you choose that wherein I am contained,
Straight shall our nuptial rites be solemnized.
But if you fail, without more speech, my lord,
You must be gone from hence immediately.
ARAGON: I am enjoined by oath to observe three things:
First, never to unfold to anyone
Which casket 'twas I chose; next, if I fail
Of the right casket, never in my life
To woo a maid in way of marriage. Lastly,
If I do fail in fortune of my choice,
Immediately to leave you and be gone.
PORTIA: To these injunctions every one doth swear
That comes to hazard for my worthless self.
ARAGON: And so have I addressed me. Fortune now
To my heart's hope! Gold, silver, and base lead.
'Who chooseth me must give and hazard all he hath.'
You shall look fairer ere I give or hazard.
What says the golden chest? Ha! Let me see:
'Who chooseth me shall gain what many men desire.'
What many men desire! That 'many' may be meant
By the fool multitude that choose by show. [...]
I will not choose what many men desire,
Because I will not jump with common spirits
And rank me with the barbarous multitudes.
Why then, to thee, thou silver treasure house.
Tell me once more what title thou dost bear:
'Who chooseth me shall get as much as he deserves.'
And well said too, for who shall go about
To cozen fortune and be honourable
Without the stamp of merit? Let none presume
To wear an undeservèd dignity. [...]
'Who chooseth me shall get as much as he deserves.'
I will assume desert. Give me a key for this,
And instantly unlock my fortunes here.

ARAGON *opens the silver casket.*

40 *blinking idiot:* weak-eyed fool
41 *schedule:* a piece of paper with writing on it
43 *deservings:* what I deserve
46 *deserts:* what I deserve
47 *distinct offices:* things that have nothing to do with each other
54 *iwis:* certainly
55 *silvered o'er:* covered in silver (i.e. lacking substance)
57 *ever:* always
be your head: be what you look like (i.e. foolish)
58 *sped:* sent away; finished
60 *linger:* stay
64 *wroth:* misery, anger
65 *singed:* burned
66 *deliberate:* carefully polite
67 their poor understanding leads them to even poorer judgement
68 *is no heresy:* is quite true
69 *hanging:* dying
wiving: finding a wife
goes by destiny: is a matter of chance
71 *what would my lord?:* what do you want?
72 *alighted:* got down from a horse/carriage

PORTIA: Too long a pause for that which you find there.
ARAGON: What's here? The portrait of a blinking idiot,
Presenting me a schedule! I will read it.
How much unlike art thou to Portia!
How much unlike my hopes and my deservings!
'Who chooseth me shall have as much as he deserves.'
Did I deserve no more than a fool's head?
Is that my prize? Are my deserts no better?
PORTIA: To offend, and judge, are distinct offices
And of opposèd natures.
ARAGON: What is here?
'The fire seven times tried this;
Seven times tried that judgement is
That did never choose amiss.
Some there be that shadows kiss;
Such have but a shadow's bliss.
There be fools alive iwis,
Silvered o'er; and so was this.
Take what wife you will to bed,
I will ever be your head.
So be gone: you are sped.'
Still more fool I shall appear
By the time I linger here.
With one fool's head I came to woo,
But I go away with two.
Sweet, adieu. I'll keep my oath,
Patiently to bear my wroth.

Exeunt ARAGON *and train.*

PORTIA: Thus hath the candle singed the moth.
O, these deliberate fools! When they do choose,
They have the wisdom by their wit to lose.
NERISSA: The ancient saying is no heresy:
'Hanging and wiving goes by destiny.'
PORTIA: Come, draw the curtain, Nerissa.

Enter a SERVANT.

SERVANT: Where is my lady?
PORTIA: Here. What would my lord?
SERVANT: Madam, there is alighted at your gate
A young Venetian, one that comes before

74 *signify:* announce

75 *sensible:* substantial
regreets: greetings/presents

76 *to wit:* that is to say, namely
commends: well-mannered compliments
courteous breath: elegant words

77 *yet:* until now

80 *costly:* of great value

81 *forespurrer:* messenger

83 *anon:* now
kin to thee: a relative of yours

84 *highday wit:* extravagant language

86 *Cupid:* (in Roman mythology) the god of love
post: messenger
mannerly: with such good manners

87 *if thy will it be:* if it is your will

To signify the approaching of his lord,
From whom he bringeth sensible regreets:
To wit, besides commends and courteous breath,
Gifts of rich value. Yet I have not seen
So likely an ambassador of love.
A day in April never came so sweet,
To show how costly summer was at hand,
As this forespurrer comes before his lord.

PORTIA: No more, I pray thee. I am half afeared
Thou wilt say anon he is some kin to thee,
Thou spend'st such highday wit in praising him.
Come, come, Nerissa; for I long to see
Quick Cupid's post that comes so mannerly.

NERISSA: Bassanio, lord Love, if thy will it be!

Exeunt.

1 Listing

List the three things that each suitor swears to do if he fails to choose the right casket:

1. ______________________________

2. ______________________________

3. ______________________________

2 Multiple Choice

Choose one of these three as best summing up the lesson of the silver casket:

- ☐ If you think you deserve the best because you are so great, then you are little more than a fool.
- ☐ Silver is the choice of those who want what everyone else wants.
- ☐ If you choose silver, it means you are prepared to risk everything for love.

3 Assess the Prince of Aragon's character from what he says in this scene and compare him to his rival, the Prince of Morocco.

4 Imagine Portia standing at her father's grave and thinking about the casket test and the suitors who have taken it until now. What might she say?

Summary

Shylock expresses his grief at the loss of his daughter and reproaches two Christian merchants, Solanio and Salerio, for being involved in her flight. He criticizes Antonio's behaviour and talks about the Jews' humanity. When his friend Tubal arrives, he is ecstatic to hear that Antonio might not be able to pay his debt back in time and devastated when he learns how much of his money Jessica has spent on trivial things.

Notes and annotations

2 *flight:* running away, escape
4 *withal:* with which
5 *fledged:* already covered with feathers, i.e. ready for flight
6 *complexion:* nature
dam: mother
8 *devil:* (here) Shylock
10 *out upon it:* to hell with it
carrion: rotten old flesh
– Salanio implies that Shylock has lost control of his old body.
14 *bad match:* business in which money is lost
bankrupt: a businessman who can't pay his debts
prodigal: someone who spends money extravagantly
14–15 *who dare scarce show his head:* who is afraid of appearing in public
15–16 *so smug upon the mart:* so clever in the marketplace
17 *he was wont to:* he used to
17–18 *for a Christian courtesy:* out of kindness
19 *forfeit:* not fulfil the terms of the contract
21 *bait fish withal:* catch fish with it
22 *hindered me half a million:* he has stopped me making half a million ducats
23 *mocked at my gains:* made fun of my profits
scorned my nation: laughed at my people (i.e. the Jews)
thwarted my bargains: prevented my business deals
24 *heated mine enemies:* made my enemies even more hostile
25 *dimensions:* parts of the body
26 *affections:* things one loves and hates
27 *subject to:* vulnerable to
means: methods
29 *prick:* wound with a sharp object
30 *wrong:* do harm to, insult
32 *humility:* kind response
32–33 *what should his sufferance be:* how should he deal with it
33 *villainy:* wickedness, evil
34 *I will execute:* I will carry out myself
it shall go hard: it will happen even if with difficulty
34–35 *I will better the instruction:* I will improve on what I have learned

Act III, Scene 1

Venice: a street

SOLANIO *and* SALERIO

Solanio and Salerio, two friends of Antonio, discuss a rumour that one of Antonio's ships has been wrecked at sea.

Enter SHYLOCK.

SOLANIO: How now, Shylock! What news among the merchants?

SHYLOCK: You knew, none so well, none so well as you, of my daughter's flight.

SALERIO: That's certain. I, for my part, knew the tailor that made the wings she flew withal.

SOLANIO: And Shylock, for his own part, knew the bird was fledged, and then it is the complexion of them all to leave the dam.

SHYLOCK: She is damned for it.

SOLANIO: That's certain, if the devil may be her judge.

SHYLOCK: My own flesh and blood to rebel!

SOLANIO: Out upon it, old carrion! Rebels it at these years?

SHYLOCK: I say my daughter is my flesh and blood.

SALERIO: [...] But tell us, do you hear whether Antonio have had any loss at sea or no?

SHYLOCK: There I have another bad match: a bankrupt, a prodigal, who dare scarce show his head on the Rialto; a beggar, that was used to come so smug upon the mart; let him look to his bond: he was wont to call me usurer; let him look to his bond: he was wont to lend money for a Christian courtesy; let him look to his bond.

SALERIO: Why, I am sure, if he forfeit, thou wilt not take his flesh: what's that good for?

SHYLOCK: To bait fish withal; if it will feed nothing else, it will feed my revenge. He hath disgraced me, and hindered me half a million; laughed at my losses, mocked at my gains, scorned my nation, thwarted my bargains, cooled my friends, heated mine enemies; and what's his reason? I am a Jew. Hath not a Jew eyes? Hath not a Jew hands, organs, dimensions, senses, affections, passions? Fed with the same food, hurt with the same weapons, subject to the same diseases, healed by the same means, warmed and cooled by the same winter and summer as a Christian is? If you prick us, do we not bleed? If you tickle us, do we not laugh? If you poison us, do we not die? And if you wrong us, shall we not revenge? If we are like you in the rest, we will resemble you in that. If a Jew wrong a Christian, what is his humility? Revenge. If a Christian wrong a Jew, what should his sufferance be by Christian example? Why, revenge. The villainy you teach me, I will execute, and it shall go hard but I will better the instruction.

Enter a SERVANT.

38 *up and down:* everywhere

39 *another of the tribe:* another Jew

cannot be matched: cannot be found to equal these two

41 *how now:* hello

43 *I often came:* I was often in places

45 *curse:* Fluch

Note, ll. 45–47: Shylock exaggerates by saying his own losses outweigh all the other terrible things that have happened to the Jewish people

47 *precious:* of great value

48 *would she were hearsed:* I wish she were lying dead in a coffin

49–50 *what's spent in the search:* how much looking for her will cost me

51 *satisfaction:* Wiedergutmachung

50–52 *nor no ill luck stirring but what lights on my shoulders:* there is no bad luck that will not land on my shoulders

52 *no sighs but of my breathing:* only I sigh of grief and sorrow

52–53 *no tears but of my shedding:* there are no tears except my own

SERVANT: Gentlemen, my master Antonio is at his house and desires to speak with you both.

SALERIO: We have been up and down to seek him.

Enter TUBAL.

SOLANIO: Here comes another of the tribe; a third cannot be matched, unless the devil himself turn Jew.

Exeunt SOLANIO, SALERIO, *and* SERVANT.

SHYLOCK: How now, Tubal! What news from Genoa? Hast thou found my daughter?

TUBAL: I often came where I did hear of her, but cannot find her.

SHYLOCK: Why, there, there, there, there! A diamond gone, cost me two thousand ducats in Frankfurt! The curse never fell upon our nation till now. I never felt it till now: two thousand ducats in that; and other precious, precious jewels. I would my daughter were dead at my foot, and the jewels in her ear! Would she were hearsed at my foot, and the ducats in her coffin! No news of them? Why so? And I know not what's spent in the search; why, thou loss upon loss! The thief gone with so much, and so much to find the thief; and no satisfaction, no revenge: nor no ill luck stirring but what lights on my shoulders; no sighs but of my breathing; no tears but of my shedding.

TUBAL: Yes, other men have ill luck too: Antonio, as I heard in Genoa –

56 *argosy:* ship
cast away: wrecked, sunk
61 *fourscore:* four times twenty, i.e. eighty
63 *dagger:* knife
64 *at a sitting:* in one evening
65 *divers:* several
creditors: Gläubiger
66 *he cannot choose but break:* he has no alternative to going bankrupt
67 *plague:* peinigen
68 *for:* in exchange for
69 *out upon her:* damn her
turquoise: Türkis
71 *Leah:* Shylock's dead wife
bachelor: an unmarried man
72 *wilderness:* a large number
73 *undone:* finished, ruined
74 *fee me an officer:* hire an officer (to arrest him) for me
75 *bespeak him a fortnight before:* engage him two weeks before the bond is due
76 *I can make what merchandise I will:* I can whatever business I want

SHYLOCK: What, what, what? Ill luck, ill luck?

TUBAL: Hath an argosy cast away, coming from Tripolis.

SHYLOCK: I thank God, I thank God. Is't true, is't true?

TUBAL: I spoke with some of the sailors that escaped the wreck.

SHYLOCK: I thank thee, good Tubal: good news, good news! Ha, ha! Heard in Genoa?

TUBAL: Your daughter spent in Genoa, as I heard, in one night fourscore ducats.

SHYLOCK: Thou stick'st a dagger in me: I shall never see my gold again; fourscore ducats at a sitting! Fourscore ducats!

TUBAL: There came divers of Antonio's creditors in my company to Venice, that swear, he cannot choose but break.

SHYLOCK: I am very glad of it. I'll plague him; I'll torture him. I am glad of it.

TUBAL: One of them showed me a ring that he had of your daughter for a monkey.

SHYLOCK: Out upon her! Thou torturest me, Tubal. It was my turquoise. I had it of Leah when I was a bachelor. I would not have given it for a wilderness of monkeys.

TUBAL: But Antonio is certainly undone.

SHYLOCK: Nay, that's true, that's very true. Go, Tubal, fee me an officer; bespeak him a fortnight before. I will have the heart of him, if he forfeit; for, were he out of Venice, I can make what merchandise I will. Go, go, Tubal, and meet me at our synagogue; go, good Tubal; at our synagogue, Tubal.

Exeunt.

1 Listing

List the pieces of good news and bad news for Shylock.

good news	bad news

2 a) Write down what Salerio and Solanio report to Antonio about Shylock's behaviour.

b) Write down what Tubal tells the other Jews at the synagogue about his meeting with Shylock.

3 Read Shylock's speech in ll. 21–35.

a) In groups, analyse the rhetorical means Shylock uses in the text and describe their effect on the audience.

b) In your group, think of ways of presenting this speech to the class; it need not be presented as a straight-forward one-man speech, but as a group effort.

c) In class evaluate why this speech is so famous.

Summary

Bassanio arrives with his friend Gratiano in Belmont and chooses the lead casket. He and Portia are in love with each other and very happy about the outcome. However, when merchants arrive with a letter from Venice, Bassanio learns that Antonio's ships have been wrecked and his debt to Shylock cannot be repaid. Portia gives Bassanio the money needed and sends him away to help his friend.

Notes and annotations

1 *tarry:* take your time
2 *hazard:* take your chance with the caskets
3 *forbear awhile:* wait a while
5 *I would not:* I do not want to
6 it is not because I dislike you that I say this
7 *but lest:* but in case
8 and a young woman is not allowed to say what she thinks
9 *detain:* keep
10 *venture for me:* try to win me
11 *am forsworn:* will have broken my promise
12 *so will I never be:* I will never be such a person
miss: lose
13–14 *wish a sin, that I had been forsworn:* wish that I had committed the sin of breaking my promise
14 *beshrew:* curse, blame
15 *o'erlooked:* bewitched, put a spell on
18 *naughty:* terrible
19 *bars:* obstacles
22 *peise:* weigh sth. down so that it cannot move
23 *eke:* make longer
24 *to stay you from election:* to prevent you from choosing
25 *I live upon the rack:* I am suffering greatly (*rack*: Folterbank)
28 *the very sum of my confession:* everything that I want to admit to
30 *deliverance:* freedom from pain/torture
34 *aloof:* at a distance
35 *sound:* be played
Note, l. 36: It was believed that swans sang once before they died
38 outward appearances may show very little of the value of what is inside
39 *still:* always
deceived with: misled by, fooled by

Act III, Scene 2

Belmont.

Enter BASSANIO, PORTIA, GRATIANO, NERISSA, *and attendants.*

PORTIA: I pray you, tarry. Pause a day or two
Before you hazard; for, in choosing wrong,
I lose your company. Therefore forbear awhile.
There's something tells me, but it is not love,
I would not lose you; and you know yourself,
Hate counsels not in such a quality.
But lest you should not understand me well –
And yet a maiden hath no tongue but thought –
I would detain you here some month or two
Before you venture for me. I could teach you
How to choose right, but I am then forsworn.
So will I never be, so may you miss me.
But if you do, you'll make me wish a sin,
That I had been forsworn. Beshrew your eyes,
They have o'erlooked me and divided me;
One half of me is yours, the other half yours,
Mine own, I would say; but if mine, then yours,
And so all yours. O, these naughty times
Put bars between the owners and their rights!
And so, though yours, not yours. Prove it so,
Let fortune go to hell for it, not I.
I speak too long; but 'tis to peise the time,
To eke it and to draw it out in length,
To stay you from election.

BASSANIO: Let me choose
For as I am, I live upon the rack. [...]
Promise me life, and I'll confess the truth.

PORTIA: Well then, confess and live.

BASSANIO: 'Confess and love'
Had been the very sum of my confession.
O happy torment, when my torturer
Doth teach me answers for deliverance!
But let me to my fortune and the caskets.

PORTIA: Away, then! I am locked in one of them.
If you do love me, you will find me out.
Nerissa and the rest, stand all aloof.
Let music sound while he doth make his choice;
Then, if he lose, he makes a swan-like end,
Fading in music. [...]

BASSANIO: So may the outward shows be least themselves.
The world is still deceived with ornament.

40 *plea:* (im Gerichtssaal) Einrede
tainted: wrong

41 *seasoned:* presented

43 *guiled:* dangerous

44 *beauteous:* beautiful

45 *veiling:* covering

Note, l. 45: 'Indian beauty' is a contradiction in terms here, as in Elizabethan times dark skin was not viewed as beautiful.

46 *the seeming truth:* a truth in appearance only
cunning: trügerisch
put on: dress up in

47 *entrap:* eine Falle stellen
gaudy: grell, knallig

Note, l. 48: The mythological King Midas was able to turn everything he touched to gold, which made it impossible for him to eat food.

48 *will:* will have, want

49 *common drudge:* thing used in servile work
– Bassanio is referring to silver, which was used for knives, forks, etc.

50 *meagre:* of little value

51 *aught:* anything

54 *fleet to air:* dissolve into air

55 *as:* such as, for example
rash-embraced: accepted too easily

56 *shuddering:* that makes you shake/tremble

Note, l. 56: Jealousy is traditionally associated with the colour green.

57 *be moderate:* relax
allay: reduce

58 *in measure rein thy joy:* with moderation control your joy
scant this excess: limit the extravagance (of emotion)

59 *thy blessing:* your gift of happiness

60 *for fear that I surfeit:* in case I become ill due to too much (happiness)

61 *counterfeit:* picture, painting
demi-god: half-god, half-human

62 *hath come so near creation:* appears so like the real person

63 *riding on the balls of mine:* being reflected in my own eyes

64 *severed:* half-opened

65 *parted with:* opened up by
bar: a tool to force things open

66 *sunder:* divide, separate
friends: (here) her lips

67 *plays the spider:* has behaved like a spider
woven: gewoben

68 *mesh:* net
entrap: catch

69 *gnats:* insects
cobwebs: Spinnennetze
scroll: a letter in the form of a paper roll

70 *continent:* thing which contains something

In law, what plea so tainted and corrupt,
But, being seasoned with a gracious voice,
Obscures the show of evil? [...]
Thus ornament is but the guilèd shore
To a most dangerous sea; the beauteous scarf
Veiling an Indian beauty; in a word,
The seeming truth which cunning times put on
To entrap the wisest. Therefore, thou gaudy gold,
Hard food for Midas, I will none of thee;
Nor none of thee, thou pale and common drudge
'Tween man and man: but thou, thou meagre lead,
Which rather threatenest than dost promise aught,
Thy paleness moves me more than eloquence;
And here choose I; joy be the consequence!

PORTIA: *[Aside]* How all the other passions fleet to air,
As doubtful thoughts, and rash-embraced despair,
And shuddering fear, and green-eyed jealousy! O love,
Be moderate; allay thy ecstasy,
In measure rein thy joy; scant this excess.
I feel too much thy blessing: make it less,
For fear that I surfeit.

BASSANIO: What find I here?

Opening the leaden casket.

Fair Portia's counterfeit! What demi-god
Hath come so near creation? Move these eyes?
Or whether, riding on the balls of mine,
Seem they in motion? Here are severed lips,
Parted with sugar breath: so sweet a bar
Should sunder such sweet friends. Here in her hairs
The painter plays the spider and hath woven
A golden mesh to entrap the hearts of men,
Faster than gnats in cobwebs. [...] Here's the scroll,

71 *that choose not by the view:* who does not choose by outward appearance
72 take a risk and choose well
74 *seek:* look for
76 and believe that your good luck will bring you happiness
78 *claim:* beanspruchen
79 *by your leave:* with your permission
80 *by note:* according to what the scroll orders me to do
to give and receive: (here) to kiss and be kissed
81 *contending:* competing in a contest
83 *universal shout:* everybody shouting
84 *giddy:* dizzy
gazing in a doubt: looking as if you cannot believe sth.
85 *peals:* loud sounds
praise: Lob
86 *thrice:* three times
even so: exactly
87 *as doubtful:* as disbelieving
91 *ambitious:* ehrgeizig
93 *trebled twenty times:* sixty times
95 *that only to:* and all this just to
account: opinion
96 *virtue:* Tugend
livings: property
97 *exceed account:* be greater than what is expected
98 *to term in gross:* to name the full total
99 *unlessoned:* uneducated
unpractised: inexperienced
100 *happy in this:* luckily
102 *not bred so dull:* not born stupid
104 *commits itself:* sich einlassen, sich ergeben
107 *converted:* given over, changed
but now: up to this moment
108 *mansion:* large elegant house
113 *presage:* ankündigen
114 *vantage:* opportunity
exclaim on you: denounce you
115 *bereft me:* taken away from me
Note, l. 116: Bassanio is blushing.
116 *veins:* Venen

The continent and summary of my fortune.
'You that choose not by the view,
Chance as fair and choose as true!
Since this fortune falls to you,
Be content and seek no new,
If you be well pleased with this
And hold your fortune for your bliss,
Turn you where your lady is
And claim her with a loving kiss.'
A gentle scroll. Fair lady, by your leave;
I come by note, to give and to receive.
Like one of two contending in a prize,
That thinks he hath done well in people's eyes,
Hearing applause and universal shout,
Giddy in spirit, still gazing in a doubt
Whether these peals of praise be his or no;
So, thrice-fair lady, stand I, even so;
As doubtful whether what I see be true,
Until confirmed, signed, ratified by you.

PORTIA: You see me, Lord Bassanio, where I stand,
Such as I am. Though for myself alone
I would not be ambitious in my wish,
To wish myself much better; yet, for you
I would be trebled twenty times myself;
A thousand times more fair, ten thousand times more rich;
That only to stand high in your account,
I might in virtue, beauties, livings, friends,
Exceed account; but the full sum of me
Is sum of something, which, to term in gross,
Is an unlessoned girl, unschooled, unpractisèd.
Happy in this, she is not yet so old
But she may learn; happier than this,
She is not bred so dull but she can learn;
Happiest of all is that her gentle spirit
Commits itself to yours to be directed,
As from her lord, her governor, her king.
Myself and what is mine to you and yours
Is now converted; but now I was the lord
Of this fair mansion, master of my servants,
Queen o'er myself; and even now, but now,
This house, these servants and this same myself
Are yours, my lord. I give them with this ring;
Which when you part from, lose, or give away,
Let it presage the ruin of your love
And be my vantage to exclaim on you.

BASSANIO: Madam, you have bereft me of all words;
Only my blood speaks to you in my veins;

118 which, after every little bit is blended together
119 *a wild:* confusion, wilderness
save of: except for
121 *parts:* leaves
from hence: from here
122 *bold:* courageous
123 *shrewd:* harmful
yon same: that
126 *constitution:* condition, mood
constant: stable, normal
128 *with leave:* excuse me
132 *blotted:* stained/spoiled with ink
133 *did impart:* told, informed
Note, ll. 134–135: Bassanio is from a good family but has no money.
136 *told you true:* told you the truth
137 *rating myself at nothing:* saying that I had no worth
138 *braggart:* Angeber
139 *state:* financial situation
141 *engaged:* bound by contract
142 *mere:* total
143 *to feed my means:* to pay for my lifestyle
144 *as:* is like
145 *gaping:* wide open
146 *issuing:* pouring out
147 *hit:* success
149 *Barbary:* the Barbary coast in North Africa
150 *'scape:* escape, survive
merchant-marring: that destroy merchants
152 *it should appear:* it seems as if
153 *present:* ready, available
discharge the Jew: pay his debt to the Jew
155 *bear:* have

And there is such confusion in my powers, [...]
Where every something, being blent together,
Turns to a wild of nothing, save of joy,
Expressed and not expressed. But when this ring
Parts from this finger, then parts life from hence:
O, then be bold to say Bassanio's dead!

Now that Bassanio and Portia are to marry, Gratiano informs Bassanio that he wishes to get married to Nerissa, Portia's maid. They fell in love and waited to see if Bassanio would guess correctly before telling the others. Everyone is happy until Salerio, Lorenzo and Jessica arrive with a letter detailing Antonio's misfortunes.

PORTIA: There are some shrewd contents in yon same paper,
That steals the colour from Bassanio's cheek:
Some dear friend dead; else nothing in the world
Could turn so much the constitution
Of any constant man. What, worse and worse!
With leave, Bassanio: I am half yourself,
And I must freely have the half of anything
That this same paper brings you.
BASSANIO: O sweet Portia,
Here are a few of the unpleasant'st words
That ever blotted paper! Gentle lady,
When I did first impart my love to you,
I freely told you, all the wealth I had
Ran in my veins, I was a gentleman;
And then I told you true; and yet, dear lady,
Rating myself at nothing, you shall see
How much I was a braggart. When I told you
My state was nothing, I should then have told you
That I was worse than nothing; for, indeed,
I have engaged myself to a dear friend,
Engaged my friend to his mere enemy,
To feed my means. Here is a letter, lady;
The paper as the body of my friend,
And every word in it a gaping wound,
Issuing life-blood. But is it true, Salerio?
Have all his ventures failed? What, not one hit?
From Tripolis, from Mexico and England,
From Lisbon, Barbary and India?
And not one vessel 'scape the dreadful touch
Of merchant-marring rocks?
SALERIO: Not one, my lord.
Besides, it should appear, that if he had
The present money to discharge the Jew,
He would not take it. Never did I know
A creature, that did bear the shape of man,

156 *keen:* determined
greedy: gierig
confound: destroy
157 *plies:* puts pressure on
158 *doth impeach:* calls into question
159 *deny:* refuse to give
160–161 *the magnificoes of greatest port:* the most important and influential people
161 *persuaded:* argued
162 *envious plea:* harmful demand
163 *forfeiture:* penalty which he is owed
bond: contract
165 *his countrymen:* his fellow Jews
169 *deny not:* do not prevent it
170 *hard:* badly
173 *draws breath:* breathes
176 *deface:* cancel
177 *treble:* make three times more
180 *call me wife:* marry me
184 *petty:* small, insignificant
188 *you shall hence:* you shall leave
189 *bid your friends welcome:* invite your friends in
show a merry cheer: be in good spirits
190 *dear bought:* bought at a high price
dear: with deep feelings
192 *miscarried:* been lost, sunk
my creditors: meine Gläubiger
193 *my estate is very low:* my situation is bad
my bond … is forfeit: I failed to fulfil the contract
193–194 *since in paying it, it is impossible I should live:* paying the price will mean my death
194 *all debts are cleared between you and I:* you owe me nothing
195 *but:* only
notwithstanding: nevertheless
use your pleasure: do as you wish
196 *let not my letter:* my letter should not do persuade you either
197 *dispatch:* finish off quickly
198 *good leave:* permission
199 *make haste:* hurry
200 no bed shall be touched by me
201 and it won't be due to sleep that I am not with you

So keen and greedy to confound a man:
He plies the Duke at morning and at night,
And doth impeach the freedom of the state,
If they deny him justice: twenty merchants,
The Duke himself, and the magnificoes
Of greatest port, have all persuaded with him;
But none can drive him from the envious plea
Of forfeiture, of justice and his bond.

JESSICA: When I was with him I have heard him swear
To Tubal and to Chus, his countrymen,
That he would rather have Antonio's flesh
Than twenty times the value of the sum
That he did owe him: and I know, my lord,
If law, authority and power deny not,
It will go hard with poor Antonio.

PORTIA: Is it your dear friend that is thus in trouble?

BASSANIO: The dearest friend to me, the kindest man [...]
Than any that draws breath in Italy.

PORTIA: What sum owes he the Jew?

BASSANIO: For me three thousand ducats.

PORTIA: What, no more?
Pay him six thousand, and deface the bond;
Double six thousand, and then treble that,
Before a friend of this description
Shall lose a hair through Bassanio's fault.
First go with me to church and call me wife,
And then away to Venice to your friend;
For never shall you lie by Portia's side
With an unquiet soul. You shall have gold
To pay the petty debt twenty times over.
When it is paid, bring your true friend along.
My maid Nerissa and myself meantime
Will live as maids and widows. Come, away!
For you shall hence upon your wedding day.
Bid your friends welcome, show a merry cheer.
Since you are dear bought, I will love you dear.
But let me hear the letter of your friend.

BASSANIO: *'Sweet Bassanio, my ships have all miscarried, my creditors grow cruel, my estate is very low, my bond to the Jew is forfeit; and since in paying it, it is impossible I should live, all debts are cleared between you and I, if I might but see you at my death. Notwithstanding, use your pleasure: if your love do not persuade you to come, let not my letter.'*

PORTIA: O love, dispatch all business, and be gone!

BASSANIO: Since I have your good leave to go away,
I will make haste. But, till I come again,
No bed shall e'er be guilty of my stay,
No rest be interposer 'twixt us twain.

Exeunt.

INFOBOX Oaths

An oath is usually a promise calling upon something or someone that the oath maker considers sacred, usually God, as a witness to the binding nature of the promise. God is used to guarantee the oath taker's own honesty and integrity in the matter under question. By implication, if the oath taker fails in their sworn duties, he or she will be punished by God. It therefore implies greater care than usual in the performance of a person's duty. It must be remembered that religion played an important role in the lives of people in the 16th century, so oaths were taken very seriously. Oaths are often confused with vows, but really, a vow is a form of dedicating yourself to something, e.g. a husband and wife take a marriage vow, a nun or priest takes a vow for life. Deliberately delivering a false oath is called perjury.

In *The Merchant of Venice*, oaths are in many ways similar to binding contracts, with the difference being that contracts are made before the law, and oaths are made before God. Both are binding, and breaking them brings with it consequences.

In the play, it is worth considering the following instances of oaths:

- Aragon, like all the suitors, takes an oath before choosing the casket (II, ix, 2 and 9), which allows him to risk all for the fairest woman. Choosing correctly will give him happiness, incorrectly, misery.
- Shylock swears an oath to pursue his law suit (III, iii, 5 and IV, i, 164–165).
- Nerissa and Portia give their men their rings and make them swear never to remove them (V, i, 29–33, 45–51).

In each case, breaking a vow brings the person in question into disrepute, so that, for example, the two women must reconsider the character of their husbands.

1 **Multiple Choice**

Choose one of these three as best summing up the lesson of the lead casket:

- □ A woman who is only interested in gold and silver will never make a good wife.
- □ Outward shows often deceive the world, so by choosing the simple and honest, one chooses correctly.
- □ Lead is solid and trustworthy and useful, and so too is the person who chooses it.

2 When Bassanio chooses the lead casket, Portia reveals her state of mind in an aside (cf. 'Infobox: Aside', p. 18). Analyse how she expresses her secret feelings and compare this to the way in which she conveys her emotions in public.

3 In this scene, one of the plot strands – the choosing of the caskets – ends, but a new plot strand commences: that of the ring. Taking Bassanio's promise into consideration, speculate on obstacles that might complicate the plot.

4 Bassanio's friend Gratiano had not expected this day to be so eventful. Imagine that he is asked what happened in Belmont when he returns to Venice and he gives a full report of the happenings.

5 Imagine Bassanio is plagued by pangs of conscience concerning Antonoi's predicament. Write down a list of what his conscience tells him and how he responds to each of these elements.

6 Write Bassanio's reply to Antonio's letter.

Summary

In Venice, Antonio begs Shylock to release him from the bond but Shylock is determined to get the pound of flesh at all costs. Antonio is resigned to his fate but hopes Bassanio will be present at his trial.

Notes and annotations

- *jailer:* prison guard

1 *look to him:* guard him
tell not me of mercy: don't speak to me about mercy
3 *hear me yet:* please listen to me
6 *before thou hadst a cause:* before you had a reason to do so
7 *beware my fangs:* watch out for my teeth
9 *naughty:* worthless
art so fond: are so foolish/careless
10 *come abroad:* come out of the prison
Note, ll. 8–10: It seems as if Antonio has persuaded the jailer to let him out of jail to plead with Shylock.
12 *I'll have my bond:* I want the conditions of my contract fulfilled
14 *dull-eyed:* stupid
15 *relent:* give in
yield: give up
16 *intercessors:* those who plead for another person in trouble
18 *impenetrable cur:* merciless/hard-hearted dog
19 *kept:* lived
20 *bootless:* useless
21 *he seeks my life:* he wants me killed
22–23 I helped many people who came to me for help to escape from being in Shylock's debt
25 *grant:* allow
26 *deny:* stop, halt
the course of law: der Lauf des Gesetztes
27 *commodity:* rights and privileges
strangers: foreigners
29 *impeach:* call into question, discredit
31 *consisteth of all nations:* comes from every nation
32 *bated me:* weakened me, made me lose weight
33 *that I shall hardly spare:* that I am not likely to give
34 *bloody:* bloodthirsty
35 *pray God Bassanio come:* I hope to God that Bassanio comes

Act III, Scene 3

Venice.

Enter SHYLOCK, SOLANIO, ANTONIO, *and* JAILER.

SHYLOCK: Jailer, look to him. Tell not me of mercy.
This is the fool that lent out money gratis.
Jailer, look to him.
ANTONIO: Hear me yet, good Shylock.
SHYLOCK: I'll have my bond; speak not against my bond.
I have sworn an oath that I will have my bond.
Thou call'dst me dog before thou hadst a cause;
But, since I am a dog, beware my fangs.
The Duke shall grant me justice. I do wonder,
Thou naughty jailer, that thou art so fond
To come abroad with him at his request.
ANTONIO: I pray thee, hear me speak.
SHYLOCK: I'll have my bond; I will not hear thee speak.
I'll have my bond; and therefore speak no more.
I'll not be made a soft and dull-eyed fool,
To shake the head, relent, and sigh, and yield
To Christian intercessors. Follow not.
I'll have no speaking. I will have my bond.

Exit.

SOLANIO: It is the most impenetrable cur
That ever kept with men.
ANTONIO: Let him alone.
I'll follow him no more with bootless prayers.
He seeks my life; his reason well I know:
I oft delivered from his forfeitures
Many that have at times made moan to me;
Therefore he hates me.
SOLANIO: I am sure the Duke
Will never grant this forfeiture to hold.
ANTONIO: The Duke cannot deny the course of law.
For the commodity that strangers have
With us in Venice, if it be denied,
Will much impeach the justice of his state;
Since that the trade and profit of the city
Consisteth of all nations. Therefore, go.
These griefs and losses have so bated me,
That I shall hardly spare a pound of flesh
Tomorrow to my bloody creditor.
Well, jailer, on. Pray God Bassanio come
To see me pay his debt, and then I care not!

Exeunt.

INFOBOX The legal system in Venice

Those who do business in Venice by drawing up contracts have equality before the law and the freedom to all the rights and privileges of the Venetians – what is called here 'the freedom of the state' (III, ii, 158). Equality before the law was essential if Venice was to remain a great commercial and financial centre, as non-Venetians could feel certain that their contracts were treated as legal documents (cf. III, iii, 26–31). Shylock has had an unusual contract drawn up by a notary within the city of Venice. When Antonio, the other signatory, fails to meet his end of the contract, Shylock insists on the contract being honoured, and the penalty (the pound of flesh) being paid. He believes that the law is paramount, even if it means the death of another person. As an outsider (Jews were evidently treated as outsiders, even if they lived within the city), Shylock believes he will have equal treatment before the law (III, iii, 8).

1 True or false?

Decide whether the following statements are true (T) or false (F) and point to evidence from the text.

T F

- □ □ Shylock tells the jailer he shouldn't have allowed Antonio out of jail.
- □ □ Antonio explains to Shylock why he should allow him more time to pay back the money.
- □ □ Shylock and Antonio are convinced that the Duke will decide in their favour.
- □ □ Antonio hopes that Bassanio will save him from having to pay with his life.
- □ □ The legal system in Venice is biased towards Venetians.

2 Continue the table which you started on p. 25, task 1. Who has the advantage now?

3 Hotseating Antonio

Get into groups of three students. One of you is Antonio waiting for his trial in a prison cell, one is a lawyer working for the Duke of Venice and the other is the jailer. The lawyer and jailer ask Antonio a lot of questions about himself, his financial situation and the bond.

Summary

Shylock is finally allowed to make his claim at court, although the Duke is unwilling to decide the matter without legal assistance. Antonio is resigned to his fate of having to die since Shylock refuses to accept any amount of money offered to release him. When Portia, disguised as a lawyer, confirms that the bond is lawful, all seems lost for Antonio as Shylock is unwilling to show any mercy. However, through a particular interpretation of the law, she manages to set the merchant free and punish Shylock at the same time. After the trial, Antonio and Bassanio want to show their gratitude to Portia, who just wants a gift, but no money.

Notes and annotations

3 that you intend to carry on with this cruelty
4 *to the last hour of act:* until the last moment
5 *thou'lt show:* you will show
remorse: compassion, pity
more strange: even more unusual/exceptional
6 *apparent:* obvious
7 *exact'st the penalty:* demand punishment
9 *loose the forfeiture:* not demand the penalty
11 *forgive a moiety:* give up a large amount/portion
principal: the total sum of money owed
12 *glancing:* looking with
13 *of late:* recently
huddled: landed/crowded
15 *gentle:* merciful
16 *I have possessed:* I have informed
your grace: form of address used to a duke
purpose: intend to do
17 *Sabbath:* Saturday (day of rest for Jews)
18 *the due and forfeit of my bond:* the debt and penalty my contract guarantees
19 *deny:* refuse
let the danger light: let damage fall
20 *charter:* constitution of the state, i.e. the law of Venice
22 *a weight of carrion flesh:* a quantity of foul flesh
24 *humour:* Laune
26 *a lodged hate:* a fixed and long-standing hatred
certain: fest, unerschütterlich
loathing: disgust, antipathy, hatred
27 *bear:* feel for
follow: bestehe auf
28 *losing suit:* a court case that will lose money

Act IV, Scene 1

In Act III, Scenes 4 and 5, Portia hands over the management of her house in Belmont to Lorenzo and Jessica, telling them that she and Nerissa will stay in a monastery until her husband Bassanio returns. She secretly sends a servant with a letter to Dr Bellario of Padua, who is a famous lawyer. She wants legal advice and hopes to borrow his lawyer's robe.
Launcelot, who is now Bassanio's servant, playfully mocks Jessica for having given up her Jewishness – a sin, he tells her, for which she will go to hell. But she believes that she has been saved because her husband has converted her to Christianity.

Venice.

Enter the DUKE, ANTONIO, BASSANIO, GRATIANO, SALERIO *with others.*

In the courtroom the Duke expresses his sympathy for Antonio. He then summons Shylock into the courtroom.

Enter SHYLOCK.

DUKE: Make room, and let him stand before our face.
Shylock, the world thinks, and I think so too,
That thou but lead'st this fashion of thy malice
To the last hour of act; and then 'tis thought
Thou'lt show thy mercy and remorse more strange
Than is thy strange apparent cruelty.
And where thou now exact'st the penalty,
Which is a pound of this poor merchant's flesh,
Thou wilt not only loose the forfeiture,
But, touched with human gentleness and love,
Forgive a moiety of the principal;
Glancing an eye of pity on his losses,
That have of late so huddled on his back,
Enough to press a royal merchant down.
[...] We all expect a gentle answer, Jew.
SHYLOCK: I have possessed your grace of what I purpose;
And by our holy Sabbath have I sworn
To have the due and forfeit of my bond.
If you deny it, let the danger light
Upon your charter and your city's freedom.
You'll ask me why I rather choose to have
A weight of carrion flesh than to receive
Three thousand ducats. I'll not answer that!
But, say, it is my humour. Is it answered?
[...] So can I give no reason, nor I will not,
More than a lodged hate and a certain loathing
I bear Antonio, that I follow thus
A losing suit against him. Are you answered?

30 *current:* flow, course
31 *I am not bound to:* I do not have to
34 *offence:* anything that harms, hurts or wounds a person
35 *sting:* bite
36 *think you question with:* remember you are arguing with
38 *than which what's harder?:* and what is harder/colder than that?
39 *beseech:* ask earnestly
40 *no farther means:* no other ways
41 as quickly and simply as possible
42 *judgement:* Urteil
46 *draw:* take, accept
47 *rendering:* giving
48 *dread:* fear, be afraid of
49 *many a purchased slave:* lots of bought slaves
50 *mules:* Maultiere
51 *abject:* erbärmlich
parts: tasks, duties
56 *dearly bought:* bought at a high cost
57 *fie upon your law:* your law be damned
58 *force:* power, authority
degrees: laws
59 *stand for:* wait for, wish for
63 *stays without:* waits outside
65 *new:* just, recently
67 *good cheer:* cheer up
courage yet: don't lose hope
69 *ere:* before
70 *tainted:* diseased, contaminated
wether: castrated male sheep
flock: herd of sheep
71 *meetest for death:* most suitable to die
74 *live still:* go on living
epitaph: inscription on a gravestone, words written about a man after his death

BASSANIO: This is no answer, thou unfeeling man,
To excuse the current of thy cruelty.
SHYLOCK: I am not bound to please thee with my answers.
BASSANIO: Do all men kill the things they do not love?
SHYLOCK: Hates any man the thing he would not kill?
BASSANIO: Every offence is not a hate at first.
SHYLOCK: What, wouldst thou have a serpent sting thee twice?
ANTONIO: I pray you, think you question with the Jew. [...]
You may as well do anything most hard,
As seek to soften that – than which what's harder? –
His Jewish heart: therefore, I do beseech you,
Make no more offers, use no farther means,
But with all brief and plain conveniency
Let me have judgement and the Jew his will.
BASSANIO: For thy three thousand ducats here is six.
SHYLOCK: If every ducat in six thousand ducats
Were in six parts and every part a ducat,
I would not draw them. I would have my bond.
DUKE: How shalt thou hope for mercy, rendering none?
SHYLOCK: What judgement shall I dread, doing no wrong?
You have among you many a purchased slave,
Which, like your asses and your dogs and mules,
You use in abject and in slavish parts,
Because you bought them: shall I say to you,
Let them be free? [...] You will answer
'The slaves are ours': so do I answer you:
The pound of flesh, which I demand of him,
Is dearly bought; 'tis mine and I will have it.
If you deny me, fie upon your law!
There is no force in the decrees of Venice.
I stand for judgement. Answer: shall I have it?
DUKE: Upon my power I may dismiss this court,
Unless Bellario, a learnèd doctor,
Whom I have sent for to determine this,
Come here today.
SALERIO: My lord, here stays without
A messenger with letters from the doctor,
New come from Padua.
DUKE: Bring us the letter. Call the messenger.
BASSANIO: Good cheer, Antonio! What, man, courage yet!
The Jew shall have my flesh, blood, bones and all,
Ere thou shalt lose for me one drop of blood.
ANTONIO: I am a tainted wether of the flock,
Meetest for death; the weakest kind of fruit
Drops earliest to the ground; and so let me.
You cannot better be employed, Bassanio,
Than to live still and write mine epitaph.

• *clerk:* assistant

77 *whet:* sharpen

79 *sole:* leather bottom of a shoe

80 *keen:* sharp

81 *hangman:* executioner

bear half the keenness: be half as sharp

82 *pierce:* touch

83 *wit:* intelligence, imagination

84 *inexecrable:* cursed, hard-hearted

85 justice itself should be accused for allowing you to live

86 *rail:* shout in an abusive and insulting way

seal: Siegel

87 *but:* just, merely

offend'st: hurt, injure

88 *repair thy wit:* make use of your intelligence again

89 *cureless:* unable to be healed

for law: to represent my just case before the court

90 *commend:* recommend as being worthy

92 *he attendeth here hard by:* he is waiting here nearby

95 *courteous conduct:* polite escort

96 *meantime:* meanwhile

97 *at the receipt of:* when I got/received

98 *in loving visitation:* paying a friendly visit

99–100 *I acquainted him with:* I made known to him

100 *cause in controversy:* case in dispute

101 *he is furnished with:* he is well informed of

102 *bettered:* improved

103 *at my importunity:* at my insistence

request: demand

104 *in my stead:* instead of me

104–105 *let his lack … estimation:* don't allow his youth to prevent him from obtaining the respect that he deserves

106 *to your gracious acceptance:* to your kind and favourable reception

106–107 *whose trial shall better publish his commendation:* whose performance at the trial will show even more clearly why I recommend him

109 *I take it:* I believe

Enter NERISSA, *dressed like a lawyer's clerk.*

DUKE: Came you from Padua, from Bellario?
NERISSA: From both, my lord. Bellario greets your grace.

Presenting a letter.

BASSANIO: Why dost thou whet thy knife so earnestly?
SHYLOCK: To cut the forfeiture from that bankrupt there.
GRATIANO: Not on thy sole, but on thy soul, harsh Jew,
Thou mak'st thy knife keen; but no metal can,
No, not the hangman's axe, bear half the keenness
Of thy sharp envy. Can no prayers pierce thee?
SHYLOCK: No, none that thou hast wit enough to make.
GRATIANO: O, be thou damned, inexecrable dog!
And for thy life let justice be accused. [...]
SHYLOCK: Till thou canst rail the seal from off my bond,
Thou but offend'st thy lungs to speak so loud:
Repair thy wit, good youth, or it will fall
To cureless ruin. I stand here for law.
DUKE: This letter from Bellario doth commend
A young and learned doctor to our court.
Where is he?
NERISSA: He attendeth here hard by,
To know your answer, whether you'll admit him.
DUKE: With all my heart. Some three or four of you
Go give him courteous conduct to this place.

Exeunt attendants.

Meantime the court shall hear Bellario's letter.
CLERK: *[Reads] 'Your grace shall understand that at the receipt of your letter I am very sick: but in the instant that your messenger came, in loving visitation was with me a young doctor of Rome; his name is Balthasar. I acquainted him with the cause in controversy between the Jew and Antonio the merchant. We turned o'er many books together. He is furnished with my opinion, which, bettered with his own learning, the greatness whereof I cannot enough commend, comes with him, at my importunity, to fill up your grace's request in my stead. I beseech you, let his lack of years be no impediment to let him lack a reverend estimation, for I never knew so young a body with so old a head. I leave him to your gracious acceptance, whose trial shall better publish his commendation.'*
DUKE: You hear the learnèd Bellario, what he writes.
And here, I take it, is the doctor come.

Enter PORTIA, *dressed like a doctor of laws.*

Give me your hand. Come you from old Bellario?
PORTIA: I did, my lord.
DUKE: You are welcome: take your place.

112 *acquainted with the difference:* informed of/familiar with the dispute between the two men

113 which is at the centre of this current case in court

114 *throughly:* thoroughly, completely

cause: subject matter

116 *stand forth:* come forward

118 *suit:* the legal action

119 *yet in such rule that:* but the suit is in order so that

120 *impugn:* oppose, find fault with

121 *you stand within his danger:* you are in danger of receiving punishment from him

122 *confess:* admit to be true

123 *merciful:* ready to forgive

124 *on what compulsion:* for what reason

125 *strained:* forced

127 *beneath:* below

blest: gesegnet

129 *mightiest:* most powerful

becomes: passt zu

131 *temporal:* earthly

132 *attribute:* essential nature, quality

awe [ɔ:]: Ehrfurcht

133 *dread:* reverence, fear

134 *this sceptred sway:* this royal rule

137 *doth then show likest God's:* then appears like God's power

138 *seasons:* makes it less harsh/severe

139 *thy plea:* what you want

140 *in the course of justice:* if we were merely dependent on justice

141 *salvation:* Erlösung

– Portia is saying that if we merely relied on God's justice, nobody would go to heaven, as people are sinners. It is due to God's mercy that people are saved (= erlöst) and go to heaven.

142 *that same prayer:* a reference to the Lord's Prayer (= das Vaterunser)

143 *deeds:* actions

144 *my deeds upon my head:* I am responsible for my actions

crave: demand, desire

146 *discharge:* pay

147 *tender:* offer

148 *suffice:* be enough

149 *bound:* prepared

152 manipulate the law for just one time so that it is subject to your authority

154 *curb of his will:* prevent from getting his way

Are you acquainted with the difference
That holds this present question in the court?

PORTIA: I am informèd throughly of the cause.
Which is the merchant here, and which the Jew?

DUKE: Antonio and old Shylock, both stand forth.

PORTIA: Is your name Shylock?

SHYLOCK: Shylock is my name.

PORTIA: Of a strange nature is the suit you follow;
Yet in such rule that the Venetian law
Cannot impugn you as you do proceed.
[To ANTONIO*]* You stand within his danger, do you not?

ANTONIO: Ay, so he says.

PORTIA: Do you confess the bond?

ANTONIO: I do.

PORTIA: Then must the Jew be merciful.

SHYLOCK: On what compulsion must I? Tell me that.

PORTIA: The quality of mercy is not strained,
It droppeth as the gentle rain from heaven
Upon the place beneath. It is twice blest:
It blesseth him that gives and him that takes.
'Tis mightiest in the mightiest: it becomes
The thronèd monarch better than his crown.
His sceptre shows the force of temporal power,
The attribute to awe and majesty,
Wherein doth sit the dread and fear of kings.
But mercy is above this sceptred sway:
It is enthronèd in the hearts of kings.
It is an attribute to God himself;
And earthly power doth then show likest God's
When mercy seasons justice. Therefore, Jew,
Though justice be thy plea, consider this,
That, in the course of justice, none of us
Should see salvation. We do pray for mercy,
And that same prayer doth teach us all to render
The deeds of mercy. [...]

SHYLOCK: My deeds upon my head! I crave the law,
The penalty and forfeit of my bond.

PORTIA: Is he not able to discharge the money?

BASSANIO: Yes, here I tender it for him in the court;
Yea, twice the sum. If that will not suffice,
I will be bound to pay it ten times o'er,
On forfeit of my hands, my head, my heart.
[...] And I beseech you,
Wrest once the law to your authority:
To do a great right, do a little wrong,
And curb this cruel devil of his will.

PORTIA: It must not be; there is no power in Venice

156 *alter:* change
a decree established: a law that has been passed
157 *'twill:* it will
precedent: Präzedenzfall
162 *most reverend:* term of address to a judge or priest
163 *thrice:* three times
165 *perjury:* the crime of swearing a false oath
166 *the bond is forfeit:* this contract is lost by failing to meet its conditions
170 *tear:* destroy, shred
171 *proceed to judgement:* give the sentence
173 *I stay on:* I insist on
175 *why then, thus it is:* well, this is how it is
176 *bosom:* breast
178 *lay bare:* uncover
181 *balance:* a pair of scales
183 *surgeon:* doctor
on your charge: at your expense
184 *lest:* in case
185 *nominated:* stated
187 *for charity:* out of human kindness
190 *armed:* spiritually ready
192 *grieve not:* don't be sad
193 *commend me:* speak well of me
194 *the process:* manner; legal actions
195 *speak me fair in death:* speak kindly of me when I am dead
196 *bid her be judge:* let her decide
197 *a love:* a loving friend
198 *repent but you that:* just regret that

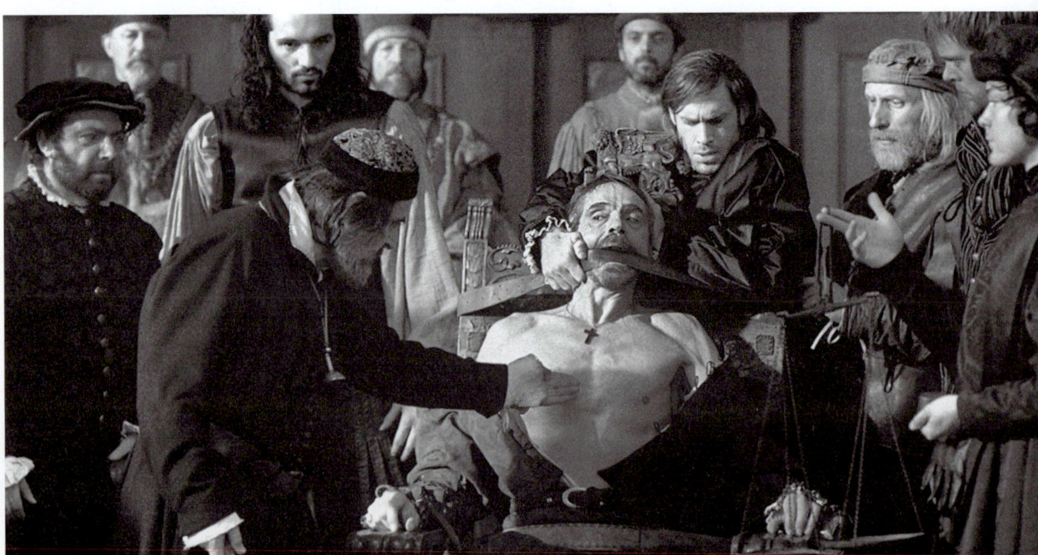

Can alter a decree establishèd:
'Twill be recorded for a precedent,
And many an error by the same example
Will rush into the state: it cannot be.
SHYLOCK: [...] O wise young judge, how I do honour thee!
PORTIA: I pray you, let me look upon the bond.
SHYLOCK: Here 'tis, most reverend doctor, here it is.
PORTIA: Shylock, there's thrice thy money offered thee.
SHYLOCK: An oath, an oath, I have an oath in heaven.
Shall I lay perjury upon my soul?
No, not for Venice.
PORTIA: Why, this bond is forfeit;
And lawfully by this the Jew may claim
A pound of flesh, to be by him cut off
Nearest the merchant's heart. Be merciful:
Take thrice thy money; bid me tear the bond.
SHYLOCK: [...] Proceed to judgement. By my soul I swear
There is no power in the tongue of man
To alter me. I stay here on my bond.
ANTONIO: Most heartily I do beseech the court
To give the judgement.
PORTIA: Why then, thus it is:
You must prepare your bosom for his knife.
SHYLOCK: O noble judge! O excellent young man! [...]
PORTIA: Therefore lay bare your bosom.
SHYLOCK: Ay, his breast:
So says the bond, doth it not, noble judge?
'Nearest his heart': those are the very words.
PORTIA: It is so. Are there balance here to weigh
The flesh?
SHYLOCK: I have them ready.
PORTIA: Have by some surgeon, Shylock, on your charge,
To stop his wounds, lest he do bleed to death.
SHYLOCK: Is it so nominated in the bond?
PORTIA: It is not so expressed, but what of that?
'Twere good you do so much for charity.
SHYLOCK: I cannot find it: 'tis not in the bond.
PORTIA: You, merchant, have you anything to say?
ANTONIO: But little: I am armed and well prepared.
Give me your hand, Bassanio: fare you well!
Grieve not that I am fallen to this for you.
[...] Commend me to your honourable wife.
Tell her the process of Antonio's end;
Say how I loved you, speak me fair in death;
And, when the tale is told, bid her be judge
Whether Bassanio had not once a love.
Repent but you that you shall lose your friend,

203 *which:* who

205 *esteemed:* valued

206 *sacrifice:* opfern

207 *deliver:* set free, save

209 *by:* nearby

210 *protest:* insist

212 *entreat:* ask earnestly, beg, urge

currish: dog-like

214 *would make else:* would otherwise

215 *these be:* this is what … are like

216 *the stock of Barrabas:* people descended from the thief released by Pontius Pilate instead of Jesus (cf. Bible, Mark 15:6)

218 *trifle:* waste

pursue: continue

sentence: Urteil

220 *awards:* gives

221 *rightful:* fair, just

225 *tarry a little:* wait a moment

226 *jot:* very small amount

227 *expressly:* clearly

229 *shed:* vergießen

231 *confiscate:* taken away by the state of Venice

232 *upright:* just and honest

233 *mark:* take notice

234 *act:* act of law

235 *urgest:* demand

240 *soft:* wait

241 *all justice:* complete justice

242 *nothing but:* just

penalty: (here) the pound of flesh

And he repents not that he pays your debt;
For if the Jew do cut but deep enough,
I'll pay it presently with all my heart.

BASSANIO: Antonio, I am married to a wife
Which is as dear to me as life itself;
But life itself, my wife, and all the world,
Are not with me esteemed above thy life.
I would lose all, ay, sacrifice them all
Here to this devil, to deliver you.

PORTIA: Your wife would give you little thanks for that,
If she were by, to hear you make the offer.

GRATIANO: I have a wife, whom, I protest, I love:
I would she were in heaven, so she could
Entreat some power to change this currish Jew.

NERISSA: 'Tis well you offer it behind her back;
The wish would make else an unquiet house.

SHYLOCK: *[Aside]* These be the Christian husbands. I have a daughter:
Would any of the stock of Barrabas
Had been her husband rather than a Christian!
We trifle time: I pray thee, pursue sentence.

PORTIA: A pound of that same merchant's flesh is thine.
The court awards it, and the law doth give it.

SHYLOCK: Most rightful judge!

PORTIA: And you must cut this flesh from off his breast:
The law allows it, and the court awards it.

SHYLOCK: Most learnèd judge! A sentence! Come, prepare!

PORTIA: Tarry a little; there is something else.
This bond doth give thee here no jot of blood;
The words expressly are 'a pound of flesh'.
Take then thy bond, take thou thy pound of flesh;
But, in the cutting it, if thou dost shed
One drop of Christian blood, thy lands and goods
Are, by the laws of Venice, confiscate
Unto the state of Venice.

GRATIANO: O upright judge!
Mark, Jew: O learnèd judge!

SHYLOCK: Is that the law?

PORTIA: Thyself shalt see the act.
For, as thou urgest justice, be assured
Thou shalt have justice, more than thou desirest.

GRATIANO: O learnèd judge! Mark, Jew: a learnèd judge!

SHYLOCK: I take this offer, then; pay the bond thrice
And let the Christian go.

BASSANIO: Here is the money.

PORTIA: Soft!
The Jew shall have all justice. Soft! No haste!
He shall have nothing but the penalty.

249 *infidel:* Ungläubiger
on the hip: at a disadvantage
251 *my principal:* the sum of money I lent on interest
255 *barely:* at the very least, even
257 *at thy peril:* at your own risk
258 *the devil give him good of it:* may the only thing that comes from it be evil
259 *question:* to argue the case
260 legally there is still another case against you
261 *enacted:* laid down, written down
262 *alien:* foreigner
264 *he seek the life:* he tries to murder
265 the person who he planned to murder
266 *seize:* take
267 *the privy coffer:* the treasury (= Staatsschatz) of the state
269 *'gainst all other voice:* only the Duke's voice counts
270 *predicament:* (here) situation in which he is dependent on the mercy of the Duke
thou stand'st: you are
271 *by manifest proceeding:* from what quite clearly has happened
274 *defendant:* Angeklagter
thou hast incurred: you have brought upon yourself
275 *formerly by me rehearsed:* in the way I described earlier
276 *down therefore:* get down on your knees
277 *thou mayst have leave:* you may be allowed
278 *thy wealth being forfeit to the state:* now that your wealth has been confiscated by the state
279 *the value of a cord:* the money a rope would cost
280 *the state's charge:* at the expense of the state
281 *that:* so that
difference of our spirits: the difference between the Christian and Jewish way of thinking
282 *I pardon thee thy life:* I allow you to live
285 *humbleness:* Demut, Reue
drive unto a fine: convert into a fine (= Geldstrafe)
286 This concerns the money given to the state, not that awarded to Antonio
288 *prop:* support

GRATIANO: O Jew! An upright judge, a learnèd judge!
PORTIA: Therefore prepare thee to cut off the flesh.
Shed thou no blood, nor cut thou less nor more
But just a pound of flesh: if thou cut'st more
Or less than a just pound [...]
Thou diest and all thy goods are confiscate.
GRATIANO: [...] Now, infidel, I have you on the hip.
PORTIA: Why doth the Jew pause? Take thy forfeiture.
SHYLOCK: Give me my principal, and let me go.
BASSANIO: I have it ready for thee; here it is.
PORTIA: He hath refused it in the open court:
He shall have merely justice and his bond. [...]
SHYLOCK: Shall I not have barely my principal?
PORTIA: Thou shalt have nothing but the forfeiture,
To be so taken at thy peril, Jew.
SHYLOCK: Why, then the devil give him good of it!
I'll stay no longer question.
PORTIA: Tarry, Jew:
The law hath yet another hold on you.
It is enacted in the laws of Venice,
If it be proved against an alien
That by direct or indirect attempts
He seek the life of any citizen,
The party 'gainst the which he doth contrive
Shall seize one half his goods; the other half
Comes to the privy coffer of the state.
And the offender's life lies in the mercy
Of the Duke only, 'gainst all other voice.
In which predicament, I say, thou stand'st;
For it appears, by manifest proceeding,
That indirectly and directly too
Thou hast contrived against the very life
Of the defendant; and thou hast incurred
The danger formerly by me rehearsed.
Down therefore and beg mercy of the Duke.
GRATIANO: Beg that thou mayst have leave to hang thyself.
And yet, thy wealth being forfeit to the state,
Thou hast not left the value of a cord.
Therefore thou must be hanged at the state's charge.
DUKE: That thou shalt see the difference of our spirits,
I pardon thee thy life before thou ask it.
For half thy wealth, it is Antonio's;
The other half comes to the general state,
Which humbleness may drive unto a fine.
PORTIA: Ay, for the state, not for Antonio.
SHYLOCK: Nay, take my life and all, pardon not that.
You take my house when you do take the prop

289 *doth sustain:* holds it together
291 *render:* grant, give
292 *a halter gratis:* a rope for free
293 *so please:* if it pleases
294 *quit:* remove
295 *so:* provided
296 *in use:* treuhänderisch
298 *lately:* recently
299 *two things provided more:* on condition of two more things
favour: Milde, Nachsicht
300 *presently:* at once
301 *record a gift:* sets down in writing a present
302 *of all he dies possessed:* of everything that he owns when he dies
303 *son:* son-in-law
304 *recant:* withdraw
305 *pardon:* Begnadigung
306 *contented:* satisfied
307 *deed:* contract concerning property
308 *from hence:* from here
312 I very respectfully ask your Grace to excuse me
314 *meet:* necessary
315 *your leisure serves you not:* you don't have time
316 *gratify:* reward for his services
317 *you are much bound to him:* you owe him a lot
319 *wisdom:* Weisheit, Klugheit
acquitted: set free
320 *grievous penalties:* terrible punishment
in lieu [lju:] *whereof:* in return for which
321 *due unto:* owed to the Jew
322 with this *(withal)* we willingly *(freely)* provide *(cope)* you for all your kind *(courteous)* trouble *(pains)*
323 *stand indebted:* are in debt
324 *ever more:* forever
326 *delivering you:* by setting you free
327 *account:* consider, think
328 *was never yet:* has never been
mercenary: interested in money

That doth sustain my house; you take my life
When you do take the means whereby I live.

PORTIA: What mercy can you render him, Antonio?

GRATIANO: A halter gratis; nothing else, for God's sake.

ANTONIO: So please my lord the Duke and all the court
To quit the fine for one half of his goods,
I am content; so he will let me have
The other half in use, to render it,
Upon his death, unto the gentleman
That lately stole his daughter.
Two things provided more: that, for this favour,
He presently become a Christian;
The other, that he do record a gift,
Here in the court, of all he dies possessed,
Unto his son Lorenzo and his daughter.

DUKE: He shall do this, or else I do recant
The pardon that I late pronouncèd here.

PORTIA: Art thou contented, Jew? What dost thou say?

SHYLOCK: I am content.

PORTIA: Clerk, draw a deed of gift.

SHYLOCK: I pray you, give me leave to go from hence;
I am not well. Send the deed after me,
And I will sign it.

DUKE: Get thee gone, but do it. [...]

Exit SHYLOCK.

DUKE: Sir, I entreat you home with me to dinner.

PORTIA: I humbly do desire your grace of pardon:
I must away this night toward Padua,
And it is meet I presently set forth.

DUKE: I am sorry that your leisure serves you not.
Antonio, gratify this gentleman,
For, in my mind, you are much bound to him.

Exeunt DUKE *and his train.*

BASSANIO: Most worthy gentleman, I and my friend
Have by your wisdom been this day acquitted
Of grievous penalties; in lieu whereof,
Three thousand ducats, due unto the Jew,
We freely cope your courteous pains withal.

ANTONIO: And stand indebted, over and above,
In love and service to you ever more.

PORTIA: He is well paid that is well satisfied;
And I, delivering you, am satisfied
And therein do account myself well paid.
My mind was never yet more mercenary.
I pray you, know me when we meet again:

331 *of force I must attempt you further:* I strongly feel I must persuade you harder

332 *some remembrance of us as a tribute:* something to remind you of us as a gift of thankfulness

333 *fee:* Honorar

grant: gewähren Sie

335 *press me far:* be insistent

yield: give in

Note l. 336: Gloves in Shakespeare's day were very expensive and elaborately made, and were worn as a sign of prestige and social standing.

340 *trifle* ['treɪfəl]: a thing of no value

341 *I will not shame myself:* I'd be ashamed

343 *methinks:* I think

I have a mind to it: I want it very much

345 *dearest:* most expensive

346 *by proclamation:* durch öffentlichen Aufruf

347 *only for this pardon me:* excuse me that I cannot give this one away

348 *you are liberal in offers:* you offer things freely (but don't intend to give them)

352 *vow:* swear

354 *'scuse:* excuse

357 she would not be angry with you for long

360 the fact that he deserves a lot together with my love

361 *valued:* balanced

commandement: order, instruction

364 *make haste:* hurry up

365 *will thither:* will go there

367 *fly:* depart quickly

I wish you well, and so I take my leave.
BASSANIO: Dear sir, of force I must attempt you further:
Take some remembrance of us as a tribute,
Not as a fee. Grant me two things, I pray you,
Not to deny me, and to pardon me.
PORTIA: You press me far, and therefore I will yield.
Give me your gloves, I'll wear them for your sake;
And, for your love, I'll take this ring from you:
Do not draw back your hand; I'll take no more.
And you in love shall not deny me this.
BASSANIO: This ring, good sir, alas, it is a trifle!
I will not shame myself to give you this.
PORTIA: I will have nothing else but only this;
And now methinks I have a mind to it.
BASSANIO: There's more depends on this than on the value.
The dearest ring in Venice will I give you,
And find it out by proclamation.
Only for this, I pray you, pardon me.
PORTIA: I see, sir, you are liberal in offers.
You taught me first to beg; and now methinks
You teach me how a beggar should be answered.
BASSANIO: Good sir, this ring was given me by my wife;
And when she put it on, she made me vow
That I should neither sell nor give nor lose it.
PORTIA: That 'scuse serves many men to save their gifts.
And if your wife be not a mad woman,
And know how well I have deserved the ring,
She would not hold out enemy forever,
For giving it to me. Well, peace be with you!

Exeunt PORTIA *and* NERISSA.

ANTONIO: My Lord Bassanio, let him have the ring:
Let his deservings and my love withal
Be valued against your wife's commandèment.
BASSANIO: Go, Gratiano, run and overtake him;
Give him the ring, and bring him, if thou canst,
Unto Antonio's house. Away! Make haste!

Exit GRATIANO.

Come, you and I will thither presently;
And in the morning early will we both
Fly toward Belmont: come, Antonio.

Exeunt.

In the following scene, Gratiano catches up with Portia and Nerissa, who are still in lawyer's robes. He gives Portia the ring from Bassanio. Nerissa decides to get her husband's ring as well, which she does.

INFOBOX | **Hidden identities**

Women dressing as men and hiding their identity in order to find out some truth or aid their men is a common feature in Shakespeare's plays. Here, Portia and Nerissa must wear men's clothes and pose as a lawyer and his assistant in order to offer legal assistance to Bassanio and Antonio. In the 16th century the legal profession was not open to women, so a woman's legal advice would not have been listened to at the time. Although Portia relies on Bellario's advice, she still embodies both a lawyer and a judge in a way that is convincing. To complicate matters further as to theatrical traditions, female roles had to be played by boys on the Elizabethan stage since it was forbidden for women to be actresses. A young male actor would therefore pretend to be a woman who in turn pretends to be a man if he played Portia's part.

1 True or false?

Decide whether the following statements are true (T) or false (F) and point to evidence from the text.

T F

☐ ☐ Portia receives gifts for her legal work from both Bassanio and Antonio.

☐ ☐ Bassanio refuses to give her his ring because he thinks it not worth her services in court.

☐ ☐ Portia has an ulterior motive in asking for Bassanio's ring.

☐ ☐ Antonio values male friendship more highly than vows made to a wife.

☐ ☐ Bassanio, Antonio and Gratiano leave for Belmont immediately.

2 This scene describes the final confrontation between Antonio and Shylock.

a) Fill in the information which you started in task 1 on p. 25.

b) Look at all your findings in the three tables that summarize Antonio and Shylock's feelings, motivations and actions. Evaluate the information and compare both men.

3 Portia's speech on the quality of mercy (ll. 125–143) is one of the most famous in the play.

a) Analyse the structure and the development of Portia's argument as well as the imagery she uses.

b) Compare this speech with Shylock's justification of his desire for revenge (III, i, 21–35; cf. p. 43), and discuss which one you find more effective.

4 a) Explain why Shylock lost his case, taking into account what he is trying to achieve, why he is trying to achieve it and what he rejects in pursuing his case.

b) Discuss to what extent mercy, as described by Portia, plays a role in the sentencing of Shylock.

5 Describe the judgement handed out to Shylock, and assess whether, in your view, this judgement was appropriate. Take into account Shylock's reaction to the judgement.

6 Assess how Shakespeare creates suspense in the trial scene, by dividing the scene into sections and drawing a tension graph, which shows how events heighten and lessen suspense and create a specific atmosphere.

7 Analyse the role of cross-dressing in this scene, taking into account gender roles, and the meaning it has for the relationships between the characters (cf. 'Infobox: Hidden identities' p. 82).

8 Speculate on what the next act will be about.

9 Write a conversation between Tubal and other Jewish merchants at the synagogue about the trial and Shylock's fate.

Summary

Portia and Nerissa return to Belmont from Venice shortly before their husbands and Antonio. The two couples have a quarrel about the missing rings and the women then reveal that they were the lawyer and his assistant. Antonio feels guilty and promises that Bassanio will keep his word in future. Portia gives Antonio a letter which informs him that his ships have all safely returned and Lorenzo is given the legal document Shylock has signed. Everyone is content and they go inside to discuss everything that has happened.

Notes and annotations

1 *methinks:* I think

4 *Antipodes:* the other side of the world

Note, ll. 4–5: Bassanio is basically saying that she would light up the night so it would be as light as day.

6 *be light:* be frivolous, immoral

9 *God sort all:* God may settle everything

12 *bound:* indebted

13 *in all sense:* in every respect

14 *bound:* in prison

15 *acquitted:* freigesprochen

18 *I scant this breathing courtesy:* I put a stop to these polite words

19 *yonder:* over there

20 *in faith:* truly, really

21 *would he were gelt:* I wish he was castrated

22 *you do take it so much at heart:* you care about it so much

24 *hoop:* ring

paltry: ridiculously small

25 *posy:* motto inscribed inside a ring

26 *cutler's poetry:* bad poetry written by a knifemaker

– In Shakespeare's time, knifemakers would inscribe a rhyming couplet on the blade of the knives they made.

32 *though not for me:* even if not for my sake

vehement: strong

oaths: Schwüre

33 *respective:* respectful, considerate

Act V, Scene 1

Belmont.

Lorenzo and Jessica are alone in Portia's house and compare their own happiness to that of well-known lovers in history. They then tease each other. A servant announces Portia's imminent return, so they arrange for music to welcome her home. Portia is understandably not in the best of moods and expresses her uneasiness by describing the night.

PORTIA *and* NERISSA, LORENZO *and* JESSICA.

PORTIA: This night methinks is but the daylight sick,
It looks a little paler; 'tis a day
Such as the day is when the sun is hid.

Enter BASSANIO, ANTONIO, GRATIANO, *and their followers.*

BASSANIO: We should hold day with the Antipodes
If you would walk in absence of the sun.
PORTIA: Let me give light, but let me not be light.
For a light wife doth make a heavy husband,
And never be Bassanio so for me.
But God sort all! You are welcome home, my lord.
BASSANIO: I thank you, madam. Give welcome to my friend.
This is the man, this is Antonio,
To whom I am so infinitely bound.
PORTIA: You should in all sense be much bound to him,
For, as I hear, he was much bound for you.
ANTONIO: No more than I am well acquitted of.
PORTIA: Sir, you are very welcome to our house.
It must appear in other ways than words,
Therefore I scant this breathing courtesy.
GRATIANO: *[To* NERISSA*]* By yonder moon I swear you do me wrong.
In faith, I gave it to the judge's clerk.
Would he were gelt that had it, for my part,
Since you do take it, love, so much at heart.
PORTIA: A quarrel, ho, already! What's the matter?
GRATIANO: About a hoop of gold, a paltry ring
That she did give me, whose posy was
For all the world like cutler's poetry
Upon a knife, 'Love me, and leave me not.'
NERISSA: What talk you of the posy or the value?
You swore to me when I did give it you
That you would wear it till your hour of death
And that it should lie with you in your grave.
Though not for me, yet for your vehement oaths,
You should have been respective and have kept it.

35 *ne'er:* never

on's face: on his face

Note, l. 35: Nerissa is threatening to kill the clerk. As clerks were often very young, he says the clerk won't live to full manhood.

39 *scrubbed:* small

40 *higher:* taller

41 *prating:* talking foolishly

42 *deny:* refuse

43 *plain:* direct, open

44 *part so lightly:* give away so easily

46 *riveted with faith:* strongly fastened/locked on in love and trust

49 *I dare be sworn for him:* I would swear an oath for him

50 *pluck it:* take it off

51 *masters:* contains, controls

53 *'twere to me:* if that had happened to me

54 *why:* an exclamation of surprise or annoyance

I were best: it would be the best for me

Note, l. 55: Throughout the rest of the scene, humour is achieved through the double entendre (= Doppeldeutigkeit) on the word 'ring', which could be also understood as 'anus' or 'vagina'.

57 *unto:* to

59 *took some pains in writing:* wrote down with great care all the events in court

60 *aught:* anything else

66 *void:* empty

72 *conceive:* imagine, understand

74 *naught:* nothing

75 *abate:* weaken, lessen

displeasure: anger

76 *virtue:* special quality or meaning

77 *half her worthiness:* half the value of the woman (i.e. Portia)

Gave it a judge's clerk! No, God's my judge,
The clerk will ne'er wear hair on's face that had it.
GRATIANO: He will, and if he live to be a man.
NERISSA: Ay, if a woman live to be a man.
GRATIANO: Now, by this hand, I gave it to a youth,
A kind of boy, a little scrubbèd boy,
No higher than thyself, the judge's clerk,
A prating boy, that begged it as a fee.
I could not for my heart deny it him.
PORTIA: You were to blame, I must be plain with you,
To part so slightly with your wife's first gift,
A thing stuck on with oaths upon your finger
And so riveted with faith unto your flesh.
I gave my love a ring and made him swear
Never to part with it; and here he stands.
I dare be sworn for him he would not leave it
Nor pluck it from his finger, for the wealth
That the world masters. Now, in faith, Gratiano,
You give your wife too unkind a cause of grief;
And 'twere to me, I should be mad at it.
BASSANIO: *[Aside]* Why, I were best to cut my left hand off
And swear I lost the ring defending it.
GRATIANO: My Lord Bassanio gave his ring away
Unto the judge that begged it and indeed
Deserved it too. And then the boy, his clerk,
That took some pains in writing, he begged mine;
And neither man nor master would take aught
But the two rings.
PORTIA: What ring gave you my lord?
Not that, I hope, which you received of me.
BASSANIO: If I could add a lie unto a fault,
I would deny it; but you see my finger
Hath not the ring upon it: it is gone.
PORTIA: Even so void is your false heart of truth.
By heaven, I will ne'er come in your bed
Until I see the ring.
NERISSA: Nor I in yours
Till I again see mine.
BASSANIO: Sweet Portia,
If you did know to whom I gave the ring,
If you did know for whom I gave the ring
And would conceive for what I gave the ring
And how unwillingly I left the ring,
When naught would be accepted but the ring,
You would abate the strength of your displeasure.
PORTIA: If you had known the virtue of the ring,
Or half her worthiness that gave the ring,

78 *contain:* keep

79 *parted with:* given away

81 *I'll die for't but:* I am absolutely certain that

83 *civil doctor:* doctor of civil law

84 *which:* who

86 and allowed him to go away angry

87 even though it was he who saved the life

89 *enforced:* forced, obliged

90 *beset:* overcome, surrounded

courtesy: good manners

91 *ingratitude:* thanklessness

92 *besmear:* make dirty

93 *these blessed candles of the night:* the stars

96 *e'er:* ever

99 *liberal:* generous, immoral

103 *bedfellow:* lover

105 *take:* catch

106 *I'll mar the young clerk's pen:* I'll ruin his pen/penis

107 *the unhappy subject:* the person who is unfortunately the cause

108 *grieve not you:* do not feel sorry

notwithstanding: in spite of (the quarrels)

109 *this enforced wrong:* the wrongdoing that was forced upon me

110 *hearing:* presence

112 *Mark you but that!:* Just listen to that!

113 *he doubly sees himself:* he sees himself twice

114 *by your double self:* by the two of you

115 *an oath of credit:* an oath that can be believed

– Portia is mocking Bassanio by saying that he is swearing by his reflection in her eyes, and as she has two eyes, this makes him have two reflections, which implies there are two Bassanios (i.e. he may be two-faced) and so his oath counts for little.

nay: no

118 *did lend my body for his wealth:* offered my body for his happiness/wealth

119 *which, but for him:* which, if it had not been for the man

120 *had quite miscarried:* would have gone quite wrong/come to harm

I dare be bound again: I would agree to another bond

121 *my soul upon the forfeit:* my soul as the penalty

122 *break faith:* break his oath

advisedly: deliberately

Or your own honour to contain the ring,
You would not then have parted with the ring.
[...] Nerissa teaches me what to believe:
I'll die for't but some woman had the ring.

BASSANIO: No, by my honour, madam, by my soul,
No woman had it, but a civil doctor,
Which did refuse three thousand ducats of me
And begged the ring, the which I did deny him
And suffered him to go displeased away,
Even he that did uphold the very life
Of my dear friend. What should I say, sweet lady?
I was enforced to send it after him.
I was beset with shame and courtesy;
My honour would not let ingratitude
So much besmear it. Pardon me, good lady,
For, by these blessèd candles of the night,
Had you been there, I think you would have begged
The ring of me to give the worthy doctor.

PORTIA: Let not that doctor e'er come near my house.
Since he hath got the jewel that I loved,
And that which you did swear to keep for me,
I will become as liberal as you.
I'll not deny him anything I have,
No, not my body nor my husband's bed.
[...] Now, by mine honour, which is yet mine own,
I'll have that doctor for my bedfellow.

NERISSA: And I his clerk. [...]

GRATIANO: Well, do you so. Let not me take him, then,
For if I do, I'll mar the young clerk's pen.

ANTONIO: I am the unhappy subject of these quarrels.

PORTIA: Sir, grieve not you. You are welcome notwithstanding.

BASSANIO: Portia, forgive me this enforcèd wrong;
And, in the hearing of these many friends,
I swear to thee, even by thine own fair eyes,
Wherein I see myself –

PORTIA: Mark you but that!
In both my eyes he doubly sees himself;
In each eye, one. Swear by your double self,
And there's an oath of credit.

BASSANIO: Nay, but hear me:
Pardon this fault, and by my soul I swear
I never more will break an oath with thee.

ANTONIO: I once did lend my body for his wealth,
Which, but for him that had your husband's ring,
Had quite miscarried. I dare be bound again,
My soul upon the forfeit, that your lord
Will never more break faith advisedly.

123 *surety:* guarantee

124 *bid:* ask

128 *by:* in exchange for

lay with: slept with

131 *in lieu of* [lju:]: in return for

132 *cuckold:* the husband of an unfaithful wife

ere: before

– Gratiano wonders why their wives have been unfaithful before the men have given them reason (because they are not good in bed) to be. Neither of them have slept with their wife yet.

133 *grossly:* rudely, in a vulgar way

amazed: confused

134 *at your leisure:* when you have time

138 *witness:* say that he saw

I set forth: I left

139 *even but now:* just now

141 *in store for you:* waiting for you

142 *unseal:* open, break the seal (= Siegel)

143 *argosies:* ships

144 *are richly come:* have arrived with rich cargo

146 *chanced on:* accidentally got

dumb: speechless

Note, l. 149: Nerissa implies either that men by their nature are promiscuous and untrustworthy, or that she could not cuckold him as she does not have a penis (*means*). It must be remembered a boy is playing the role and could present these lines in a sexual way.

155 *come to road:* come into port

how now: used to get the attention of somebody

156 *good comforts:* good news

157 *without a fee:* for free

159 *a special deed of gift:* a legal document about a gift

160 *of all he dies possessed of:* of everything he owns at his death

PORTIA: Then you shall be his surety. Give him this
And bid him keep it better than the other.
ANTONIO: Here, Lord Bassanio; swear to keep this ring.
BASSANIO: By heaven, it is the same I gave the doctor!
PORTIA: I had it of him. Pardon me, Bassanio;
For, by this ring, the doctor lay with me.
NERISSA: And pardon me, my gentle Gratiano;
For that same scrubbèd boy, the doctor's clerk,
In lieu of this last night did lie with me.
GRATIANO: [...] What, are we cuckolds ere we have deserved it?
PORTIA: Speak not so grossly. You are all amazed.
Here is a letter. Read it at your leisure.
It comes from Padua, from Bellario.
There you shall find that Portia was the doctor,
Nerissa there her clerk. Lorenzo here
Shall witness I set forth as soon as you
And even but now returned. I have not yet
Entered my house. Antonio, you are welcome;
And I have better news in store for you
Than you expect. Unseal this letter soon.
There you shall find three of your argosies
Are richly come to harbour suddenly:
You shall not know by what strange accident
I chancèd on this letter.
ANTONIO: I am dumb.
BASSANIO: Were you the doctor and I knew you not?
GRATIANO: Were you the clerk that is to make me cuckold?
NERISSA: Ay, but the clerk that never means to do it,
Unless he live until he be a man.
BASSANIO: Sweet doctor, you shall be my bedfellow.
When I am absent, then lie with my wife.
ANTONIO: Sweet lady, you have given me life and living,
For here I read for certain that my ships
Are safely come to road.
PORTIA: How now, Lorenzo!
My clerk hath some good comforts too for you.
NERISSA: Ay, and I'll give them him without a fee.
There do I give to you and Jessica
From the rich Jew a special deed of gift,
After his death, of all he dies possessed of.

161 *manna:* (biblical) food God gave when the Israelites marched through the desert (Exodus 16:14 ff.)

162 *starved:* dying of hunger

163–164 *you are not satisfied of these events at full:* you want to hear more details

165–166 and ask all your questions which we will answer under oath

168 *so sore:* so intensely

LORENZO: Fair ladies, you drop manna in the way
Of starvèd people.
PORTIA: It is almost morning,
And yet I am sure you are not satisfied
Of these events at full. Let us go in,
And charge us there upon inter'gatories,
And we will answer all things faithfully.
GRATIANO: [...] Well, while I live I'll fear no other thing
So sore as keeping safe Nerissa's ring.

Exeunt.

1 Study ll. 70–79 in which Portia and Bassanio quarrel about the ring he gave away. The stylistic device of ending several lines with the same word is called 'epistrophe'. Analyse how Shakespeare makes use of it in this passage and say what effect he wanted to achieve.

2 Explain why Portia and Nerissa pretend that the 'doctor' and the 'clerk' spent the night with them.

3 Explain the significance of Antonio offering a second bond (ll. 118–122).

4 Analyse Bassanio's relationships with both Antonio and Portia, showing how they have developed over the play. Take into account the lending of money, the bond, the ring, the oaths (cf. 'Infobox: Oaths', p. 58 for more information) as well as male friendships and marriage vows.

5 Several theatre directors have cut the last act altogether and ended the play with Shylock's exit in Act IV, Scene 1. Discuss whether this does justice to the structure and the contents of the drama.

6 Evaluate the atmosphere at the end of the play, taking into account the following:

- the marriage of Bassanio and Portia
- the marriage of Gratiano and Nerissa
- the marriage of Lorenzo and Jessica
- the situation of Antonio
- the situation of Shylock

7 After Antonio returns to Venice, he writes a diary entry of his visit to Belmont, in which he reflects on what has happened and how he feels.

INFOBOX William Shakespeare

William Shakespeare (1564–1616) is widely regarded as the greatest writer in the English language. His surviving work consists of about 38 plays, 154 sonnets and several other poems. His plays are performed worldwide more often than those of any other playwright.

We know little about Shakespeare. He was born and brought up in Stratford-upon-Avon. His father was a member of the town council and a maker of gloves. At the age of 18, he married Anne Hathaway, with whom he had three children: Susanna (born 1583), and twins Hamnet and Judith (born 1585). At some point he moved to London, where by 1592 he had become known as a playwright and was beginning his acting career in the theatres of London. In 1594 a group of actors, including Shakespeare, formed the Lord Chamberlain's Men, which soon became the leading company in London. In 1599, they built their own theatre on the south bank of the River Thames, called the Globe. In 1608 the company also took over the Blackfriars indoor theatre. Records of Shakespeare's property purchases and investments indicate that the company made him a wealthy man. After the death of Queen Elizabeth in 1603, the company was awarded a royal patent by King James I, and changed its name to the King's Men.

He appears to have retired to Stratford around 1613 at the age of 49, where he died three years later. Few records of Shakespeare's private life survive, and there has been considerable speculation about such matters as his physical appearance, sexuality, religious beliefs, and whether the works attributed to him were written by others.

Shakespeare produced most of his known work between 1589 and 1613. His early plays were mainly comedies and histories (the latter concerned the history of England in the Middle Ages). Until about 1608 he wrote mainly tragedies, including *Hamlet, King Lear, Othello* and *Macbeth*. In his last phase, he wrote romances, such as *The Tempest. The Merchant of Venice* is believed to have been written between 1596 and 1598. While many of his plays were published in editions of varying quality and accuracy during his lifetime, in 1623, two of his former colleagues published the First Folio, a collected edition of his dramatic works that included all but two of the plays now recognised as Shakespeare's. His sonnets were published in 1609.

GENERAL QUESTIONS ON THE PLAY

1 Summarize the plot of *The Merchant of Venice* in no more than four sentences.

2 **a)** Explain the interrelationship of the three strands of the plot (the one dealing with the caskets, the one dealing with revenge and the one dealing with the rings).

b) Assess whether the internal structure would hold if one of them was left out.

3 **a)** Look back at the whole play and analyse the following elements of its structure stating what happens at each of these two points (cf. 'Infobox: Dramatic structure', p. 24):

– the climax of the play

– the falling action

b) Evaluate which genre of drama this play belongs to.

4 **a)** Shakespeare deals with different contrasting themes in his play, some of which are interconnected:

love – hatred

justice – mercy

appearance – reality

Create mind maps for each theme using examples taken from the play and then show its interdependence with the contrasting theme (e.g. justice versus mercy).

b) Explain the significance of money in the play for all the themes.

5 Critics have often denounced *The Merchant of Venice* as being an anti-Semitic play. Discuss whether you agree, listing all the evidence from the text and taking into account how Shakespeare's audience might have viewed it. If you wish to debate this in class, consider how a motion might be formulated.

6 Read what the eminent scholar Harold Bloom in his book *Shakespeare – the Invention of the Human* (1998) says about Portia in this quote.

'Herself a sophisticated ironist, she [Portia] settles happily for the glittering gold digger Bassanio, contemptuously sentences Morocco and Aragon to celibate existences, and is delighted with her Belmont and Venice alike. More even than the vicious Gratiano, she incarnates the "anything goes" spirit of Venice, and her quality of mercy cheerfully tricks Shylock out of his life's savings in order to enrich her friends.'

a) Discuss whether you agree or not.

b) Outline the way in which Portia interferes with the fates of the three male protagonists: Bassanio, Shylock and Antonio.

7 **a)** Discuss which of the following qualities describe the main couple, Bassanio and Portia.

		Yes	No	Somewhat
	emancipated			
	patronising			
Portia is	empathetic			
	merciful			
	self-righteous			
	powerful			
	intelligent			

		Yes	No	Somewhat
	a fortune hunter			
	careless			
Bassanio is	loyal			
	honest			
	superficial			
	selfish			
	sensitive			

b) Speculate on the future relationship between Bassanio and Portia, assessing whether Portia will be a happy wife and Bassanio a reliable husband, and evaluating where problems might arise.

8. In class, think of memorable moments in the play and do staged tableaux of some of them.

9 Imagine you are given the task to design a stage set for the play. What sort of atmosphere would you evoke in the different settings and what means would you use to create them?